Ski Touring the Red Rock Country

Ski Touring
THE RED ROCK COUNTRY

Winter Trails in Southwest Utah

Jonathan Guy Wynn

The University of Utah Press
Salt Lake City

© 2003 by The University of Utah Press
All rights reserved

08 07 06 05 04 03
5 4 3 2 1

Frontispiece photo © Nathan Wynn

Library of Congress Cataloging-in-Publication Data

Wynn, Jonathan Guy, 1969–
  Ski touring the red rock country : winter trails in southwest Utah / Jonathan Guy Wynn
    p.   cm.
Includes bibliographical references and index.
  ISBN 0-87480-739-5
  1. Cross-country skiing—Utah—Guidebooks. 2. Utah—Guidebooks.
I. Title
  GV854.5.U8 W96 2003
  917.9204'033—dc21
                                        2002007148

To the Hippos in the Bryce Canyon sky for inspiring this book

CONTENTS

Introduction

1. Skiing in the Southern Utah Desert? 1
2. The Geological History of Southwest Utah 2
3. Equipment, Safety, and Other Things You Need to Know 6

    To Ski or to Snowshoe? 6

    About Equipment 7

        Ski Equipment 7

        Snowshoe Equipment 8

        Other Winter Travel Equipment 9

    Nordic Ski Waxing 12

    Ski Techniques 14

    Weather 14

    Avalanches 15

    Other Hazards 16

    Winter First Aid 16

    Trail Etiquette 17

    Snowmobiles 18

    Access to Trailheads 18

4. How to Use this Book 19

The Ski Tours

    Area 1—Bryce Canyon and Surroundings, Including Ruby's Inn Resort: Eocene Lakes of the Paunsagunt Plateau   23

    Area 2—Cedar Breaks and Surroundings, Including Brian Head Ski Resort and Cedar Breaks National Monument: Cenozoic Plateau Building and Quaternary Volcanoes on the Markagunt Plateau   55

    Area 3—The Tushar Range, Including Elk Meadows Ski Area: Mineral Deposits and Volcanoes of the Tushar Mountains   97

    Area 4—The High Plateau Country from Boulder to Torrey: Pleistocene Ice Caps of the Aquarius, Table Cliffs, and Boulder Mountain Plateaus   127

    Area 5—The Fishlake National Forest Area Near Richfield: Tectonics and Faults on the Fish Lake Plateau   151

    Other Skiing Areas of Southwestern Utah   175

Appendix: GPS Cooordinates for Trailheads   177

Recommended Reading   180

Acknowledgments   181

About the Author   182

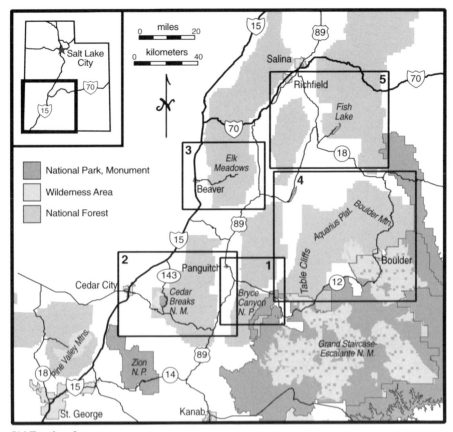

Ski Touring Areas:
1. Paunsagunt Plateau (including Bryce Canyon National Park).
2. Markagunt Plateau (including Cedar Breaks National Monument, Brian Head Ski Resort).
3. Tushar Mountains (including Elk Meadows Ski Resort).
4. Aquarius, Boulder and Table Cliffs Plateaus.
5. Fish Lake Plateau.

Introduction

1. Skiing in the Southern Utah Desert?

Mention the notion of skiing in the southern Utah "desert" to the uninitiated and you will probably get blank stares from most people, and very strange looks from a few others. Most people simply don't think of southern Utah as a winter recreation area, especially for cross-country skiers and snowshoers. Rather, southern Utah is more widely known for its great hiking, canyoneering, mountain biking, and scenic driving. A very small number of downhill and telemark skiers will probably know of the superb powder and uncrowded conditions at the local, small-town resorts of Brian Head and Elk Meadows (see Ski Touring Areas 2 and 3 of this book). However, most others—particularly non-skiers—do not realize the quantities of snow that blanket this "desert" every winter, nor do they know of the resulting beauty of skiing through the Red Rock Country.

During the summer tourist season, literally millions of recreationists flock to southwest Utah to experience the breathtaking geological scenery of recreation areas such as Bryce Canyon and Zion National Parks, Cedar Breaks and the Grand Staircase–Escalante National Monuments, Kodachrome Basin State Park, and the Dixie National Forest. Little do many of these people know that these scenes are even more spectacular when covered in a light dusting of fresh snow, under incredibly blue skies, and viewed through crisp, clean winter air. Nor is it widely known that these backcountry areas are often readily accessible on a pair of skis or snowshoes. The relatively few winter touring enthusiasts who know this "Red Rock Country" can attest that the winter experience in the southern Utah high country is unrivaled for its solitude and scenic beauty.

For many people, this book will offer an introduction to ski touring and snowshoeing in southwestern Utah, an area that is typically not thought of in terms of its winter recreation potential. For the few who have already tasted the experience of winter touring on these high plateaus, this book will offer more details on additional routes and alternative areas, as well as descriptions of the geology that makes ski touring in the Red Rock Country so spectacular.

The purpose of this book is to introduce a variety of beginner and intermediate trails to the average ski tourer unfamiliar with the range of skiable terrain in southern Utah. However, there is a great deal of untracked backcountry in the high mountainous regions near Brian Head, the Tushar Mountains, and Boulder Mountain that is very suitable for advanced backcountry, telemark, and alpine-touring skiers. This type of skiing is beyond the scope of this book, short of providing suggestions for accessing such terrain via more intermediate ski trails. Such advanced skiers should already be familiar with this backcountry, as well as familiar with the necessary route-finding and map-reading skills, and therefore have no need for a guidebook to this area.

A large part of the allure of skiing or snowshoeing through areas such as Bryce Canyon and Cedar Breaks is to be able to experience some of the red rock geology during the unusual circumstances of winter. My experience with skiing among groups at the annual Winter Festival at Bryce Canyon is that people not only want to see the beauty of the contrasting red rocks, white snow, and blue sky, they also want to be able to understand some of the geological and natural history that makes these great vistas so spectacular. Although winter touring on skis or snowshoes does not provide access to geological features at the hand-specimen or outcrop scale (because the rocks underfoot are covered by several feet of snow!), one can still gain a great appreciation of the local geological history at the much larger landscape scale. Much of the geological history can be seen and understood while touring quietly through the gentle terrain of the plateaus on skis or snowshoes. Southwest Utah is somewhat unique in this respect, because the nature of the terrain permits (and almost encourages) skiing on high plateau surfaces and canyon bottoms, which are often covered deep in snow for most of the winter. However, despite these quantities of snow, the nature of the terrain still exposes the geological scenery in the cliffs and badlands at the plateau margins.

2. The Geological History of Southwest Utah

Part of the rewarding experience of winter touring in southern Utah is the ability to negotiate some of the unique geological features during

Age	Era	Period	Events	Rocks	Ski Tours
0.01	Cenozoic	Holocene	Most recent interglacial stage, continued faulting.	Pleistocene tills and landslide deposits	Area 4, High Plateaus especially Boulder Mountain Hightop.
1.8		Pleistocene	Alternating glacial periods (ice ages) and interglacials. Glaciated high plateaus above 11,000 ft (3350 m.), continued Basin and Range faulting.		
5.3		Pliocene	Basin and Range faulting episode, major faulting in Colorado Plateaus region, dicing up flat lying rocks and uplifting the plateaus such as the Markagunt, Paunsagunt, Kolob, Sevier, Aquarius, Table Cliffs, and Boulder Mountain. Wasatch line marks current boundary of heavily faulted region.	(faulting and uplift)	Areas 2 and 5, Markagunt Plateau and Fish Lake.
		Miocene			
23.7		Oligocene	Massive stratovolcanoes forming volcanic calderas near Mt. Belknap, Delano Peak, Big John Flat, Bullion Canyon and Monroe Peak. Deposition of thick volcanic pile in Marysvale Volcanic Province. Associated alteration of bedrock by intrusive rocks, and formation of ore deposits.	Mt. Dutton Fm. Bullion Canyon volcanics	Area 3, Tushar Mtns. and Monroe Peak in Area 5.
36.6		Eocene	erosive period		
57.8			Large, flat lake systems in southwestern Utah, likely connected with Flagstaff Lake of Uinta Basin. All of southwestern Utah was a flat basin, with scattered lakes which waxed and waned with climatic cycles.	Claron Fm.	Areas 1 and 2, Bryce Canyon and Cedar Breaks and Table Cliffs in Area 4.
		Paleocene	Soil formation in river and delta systems feeding lakes, which were probably more extensive to the north.		
66.4	Mesozoic	Cretaceous	Terrestrial environment and shallow inland seas. Cretaceous interior seaway deposited drab grayish and blue rocks of the Grand Staircase region ("the Blues").	Kaiparowits Fm. Straight Cliffs Fm. Tropic Shale Dakota Fm. Morrison Fm. Entrada Ss. Carmel Fm. Navajo Ss. Chinle Fm. Moenkopi Fm.	Area 4, Pine Lake and Barney Top tours.
		Jurassic			
		Triassic			
144	Paleozoic	Permian			
		Pennsylvanian			
		Mississippian	Marine environments throughout most of Utah, little rock record preserved in soutwest.		
		Devonian			
		Ordovician			
570		Silurian			
		Cambrian			
	pre-Cambrian				

the seemingly unusual conditions of a winter landscape. In this barren desert region of rocky outcrops, the contrast of a fresh blanket of alpine snow makes skiing in the red rock landscape especially satisfying. As one wanders through the solitude imposed by the winter white, the inquisitive mind can't help but think about how these peculiar red rock landscapes came to be. After a weekend of touring through these natural wonders, even the most experienced natural scientist generally comes out with a series of questions about the regional geological and natural history. What makes the contrasts of this region so great? Why are the plateaus so high? How and why do they differ from one another? Why are some of the rocks red? Why are others not? Such natural reflections are what attracts most geologists to their field of study and keeps them interested in their environment.

Geologists most often think of Earth events first and foremost in a sequence, organized by their relative age—a geological history. Therefore, much of the geological presentation in this book is laid out with respect to the geological time scale. This introductory section provides the temporal framework for the series of geological discussions to be found in the chapters on the ski touring areas, covering for each area the salient aspects of its regional geological history and the geological features to be observed while touring there.

In general, geological features of southwestern Utah, especially those characteristic of the skiable high plateau country, are extremely young with respect to maximum age of the Earth, belonging to the Cenozoic Era (65 million years old and younger, compared to 4.55 billion years of total Earth history). The Cenozoic, the youngest of the four geological eras, is a mere blip of time compared to the age of some of the oldest rocks in the world, or even the oldest rocks in the United States. Such old rocks are particularly notable in other well-known cross-country skiing areas such as the Upper Midwest and New England, and most of Scandinavia. These older and more geologically stable landscapes generally date to the pre-Cambrian and Paleozoic Eras, a whopping swath of time from 590 to 4,550 million years ago. It is the youthfulness of the red rock landscape of southern Utah, a result of recent geological activity, that gives this high plateau country its exceptional prominence and high topographic relief.

Prior to the Cenozoic Era, most of the geological history of southern Utah is characterized by sedimentation in quiet ocean basins and inland seas. Because dissolved oxygen is depleted in deep water settings, and the processes of oxidation (similar to the process of the rusting of metal) of iron-bearing minerals are inhibited, many of these pre-Cenozoic sedimentary rocks are very drab in color. Interspersed with the gray, green, and blue Paleozoic and Mesozoic marine rocks, however, are "red bed" formations resulting from periods characterized by low global sea level. The Triassic is best known for its red beds, such as those of the Moenkopi and Chinle Formations of the Grand Staircase region.

The Cenozoic Era began a trend toward global cooling and long-term decrease in relative sea level, leading to changed sedimentary environments of southwestern Utah toward a broad depositional system of rivers, deltas, and lakes. In such dynamically changing terrestrial sedimentary systems, soil formation is common between brief periods of deposition during flooding events. This period, with its unique formation of ancient soils, gave the Cenozoic rocks their red, pink, orange, and yellow chromas, as seen in the Pink Cliffs exposures of the lower

Claron Formation at Cedar Breaks National Monument and Bryce Canyon National Park. The Claron lake was part of a more extensive system of lake basins formed during these epochs, extending all the way to the Green River Basin of northeastern Utah and southwestern Wyoming.

Following the relatively lazy interval of layer-cake sedimentation in rivers and lakes, a dramatic environmental change brought a series of immense stratovolcanoes to southwestern Utah, and resulted in massive outpourings of volcanic rocks centered around the Marysvale area. Such volcanic centers are presently known only at continental margins, such as the Andes, the Aleutians, and the Cascades, leaving the Marysvale Volcanic Province without a real modern counterpart, and something of an intriguing mystery to most igneous geologists. Extrusion and intrusion of these igneous rocks into the surrounding bedrock was accompanied by hot groundwater fluids that altered the original bedrock, sometimes beyond recognition, and formed the mineral deposits of the Marysvale and other great mining districts througout the western United States. Precious metals such as gold, silver, lead, and zinc are easily dissolved, concentrated, and reprecipitated by such solutions, which flow through the bedrock under the extreme high temperatures and pressures in volcanic districts.

With a major rearrangement of continental and oceanic plates during the Miocene Period, the Basin and Range province was born. This tectonically distinct region is best known by the elongate north-south trending mountain ranges typical of Nevada and western Utah, which currently extend to its eastern boundary at the southern high plateaus. This tectonic switch is marked by a reversal in the relative elevations of the Colorado Plateau and Basin and Range provinces, probably brought about by a mysterious increase in mantle heat flow to the Basin and Range (particularly at its margins), causing it to rise above the Colorado Plateau to the east. Uplift of the southwestern Utah plateaus to such high elevations as 11,000 ft. (3,350 m.), combined with the culmination of the Cenozoic global cooling, brought large ice sheets to cap the Aquarius Plateau, while alpine glaciers carved their way through high, craggy ranges such as the Tushar Mountains. During this, the most recent and slightly warmer Holocene Epoch (really just one phase in a cyclic pattern of glacial and interglacial periods), snow and ice persist in these regions only during winter months, when skiers find a few remnants of their former glacial glory in the form of ice-rafted boulders (erratics) and glacial moraine deposits and lakes.

3. Equipment, Safety, and Other Things You Need to Know

To Ski or to Snowshoe?

Although the trails described in this book are designed to be used by both skiers and snowshoers, it may be obvious that the author prefers winter touring by ski. That being said, each method of winter travel does have its own set of benefits and drawbacks, all of which vary with the terrain to be covered and the preference of the ski or snowshoe tourer. Both involve strapping somewhat awkward objects to your feet and trekking through deep snow. Both methods of winter travel make trekking through deep snow, an otherwise impossible task, both easy and enjoyable. It is the conditions of the snow and trail that can give one method its advantages over the other.

Although skis are useful in covering long distances, particularly in gently rolling terrain, open conditions, and modest snow depths, snowshoes have their advantages where skis fail to perform. Snowshoes are much more capable of traversing narrow sections of trail constricted by dense trees, brush, rocks, tight turns, or other obstructions to a longer pair of cross-country skis. Snowshoeing does not require the somewhat steep learning curve that skiing does, and is much easier to pick up without having any prior downhill skiing experience (it's just like walking with big shoes). The fear of excessive speed on downhills is often enough to keep some people off skis. These hills are far less scary on grippy snowshoes than on a pair of skinny skis. Extremely deep snow conditions can make trailbreaking difficult on skis, particularly narrower cross-country skis, while snowshoers may find this somewhat easier. Snowshoeing also proceeds at a slower pace, and therefore makes carrying on a pleasant conversation easier than it is while gliding past your partner on a pair of skis. Families with young children may find snowshoeing a much easier way to introduce children to winter touring sports activities.

Despite the advantages of snowshoeing, cross-country skiing has traditionally been the preferred method of traversing rolling terrain for winter sport. Perhaps it is the joy of extending that extra bit of glide between each step, being able to attain quicker speeds for the effort put in (especially on downhills), or simply doing things the way nordic skiers have been for centuries. It is the experience of gliding gently through a meadow, with the occasional kick between steps, which is certainly enough to keep the author on skis every chance available. Some would also say there is a certain grace (or maybe it's a Zen quality) to cross-country skiing that simply cannot be attained on snowshoes. Also, the faster pace of skiing does allow the skier to reach deeper into the backcountry than he/she can on snowshoes.

About Equipment

Equipment for winter touring includes the technical gear for either skiing or snowshoeing (skis or snowshoes), as well as the basic auxiliary equipment required for winter travel. Because the technology of ski and snowshoe equipment is changing rapidly, it is not the purpose of this book to provide recommendations other than to describe the general types of winter touring gear available, and to discuss which are most appropriate for the type of terrain in southwestern Utah. If you are buying or renting equipment for the first time, you should discuss with a ski outfitter the types of equipment most suited to the type of skiing you wish to pursue. If you are unfamiliar with the kinds of equipment available, be sure to try out a variety of gear before purchasing.

Ski Equipment

The variety of nordic skiing equipment available at most retailers is sometimes overwhelming. Much of the range of equipment available is often designed for specific types of skiing, and varies from heavy-duty telemark and randonee gear to skinny track-skating and racing skis. Skiing equipment best suited to most of the terrain to be experienced in southern Utah may be most appropriately called "Backcountry Ski Touring," but may otherwise be known as "Ski Touring," "Backcountry," or in some cases simply "Cross Country" skis. Because of the variety of terrain on any given trail, the most generalized rather than specialized equipment is best suited to this type of ski touring. At the light end of the range, extremely narrow and lightweight racing and light touring skis are generally inappropriate because most of the trails described in this book are not well groomed. At the other end, heavy-duty telemark gear (wider skis and heavy plastic boots) is generally overkill for most of the gentle terrain described here. This having been said, there *are* areas where specialized track skiing equipment is appropriate, such as the few groomed resorts (Bryce Canyon, Brian Head, and Elk Meadows). And there are areas where telemark gear is appropriate, such as the Brian Head downhill areas and the deeper backcountry of the Tushar Range. Whatever type of skiing you wish to pursue, make sure that your gear is most suited to that purpose.

Skis. Most suitable backcountry equipment includes skis that are neither so narrow that they are unstable in deep snow nor so wide that they are a constant burden when gliding through gentle terrain (a 68-55-62–mm. sidecut is good). In general, slightly shorter skis (5–10 cm. shorter than typical touring skis) perform better in the ungroomed conditions typical of most of southern Utah. Metal-edged skis are often useful for controlling turns and descents on the backcountry tours, especially in the crusty or icy conditions that often prevail between storms. Flex and camber are two other factors to consider. A full nordic camber (double camber) is best for improved classical striding. A moderate ski flexure allows for the maximum adaptability to the variety of terrain to be experienced. The various benefits of waxable and waxless skis are often a highly debated subject, but it comes down to a matter of personal preference. Waxless skis are suitable for most any trail in this area, and are easier to maintain. Waxable skis, when waxed and maintained properly, are a joy to ride through the southern Utah terrain. For those who still prefer waxable skis, a section on waxing skis specifically for southern Utah snow is provided later in this chapter.

Bindings. Bindings should be sturdier and more stable than ordinary light touring gear. Three-pin bindings are the most suitable, being very stable. However, they are being phased out by the modern NNN (New Nordic Norm) and the similar SNS (Salomon Nordic Norm) systems. Among NNN bindings, NNN-BC (or SNS-BC; Backcountry) bindings are more robust, and therefore most suited to the backcountry conditions typical of most of southern Utah. Those who are practicing telemark turns on steep slopes generally use three-pin bindings and benefit from the stability of an additional three-pin cable.

Boots. The key to good boots is simply comfort. They should fit snugly, be well broken in, adequately insulated, waterproof, and stiff enough to provide ample support in light backcountry conditions. If purchasing boots separately from skis and bindings, make sure that they are of the right type to fit the binding.

Poles. Poles should be sturdy, have large baskets, and be of intermediate length. Telescoping poles are preferred, because they can be extended and shortened to suit the conditions and terrain.

Snowshoe Equipment

Snowshoes. Snowshoes have come a long way in the last decade, from the old wood and rawhide "tennis rackets" to modern aluminum and synthetic types that make snowshoeing easier and more fun. The variety of equipment available ranges from small racing snowshoes to much larger shoes for overnight trekking with heavy gear.

The type of shoes you choose depends predominantly on the snow conditions you plan on using them in. The size of the snowshoe should be suited to the length of the trip, depth of snow, and weight of gear to be carried. As with skis, the intermediate equipment is best suited to the variety of conditions in southern Utah. Generally, snow depths are not extreme in this area, so the smaller end of the range is best, unless you plan on extended trips with overnight gear. Smaller shoes can make the going much easier and learning to snowshoe much more pleasant.

Boots. Just about any boot or shoe can be fitted into the binding of a snowshoe, from leather hiking boots through insulated boots to plastic mountaineering boots. However, as with ski boots, comfort is again the key. They should be waterproof, well insulated, and provide good ankle support.

Poles. Some snowshoers prefer to use poles for stability, much as many hikers have begun to use trekking poles. This is simply a matter of preference—try it both ways. The extra stability of poles may be preferred on steeper slopes and unstable conditions.

Other Winter Travel Equipment

Clothing. Clothing is the most basic equipment necessary for any type of winter touring. Your enjoyment and comfort will depend almost entirely on what you wear and how well it suits the weather conditions. Most people who have become disillusioned with cross-country skiing have done so because of poor clothing, or poorly suited clothing. These clothing mistakes generally result in the "isn't cross-country skiing so much *work*" and the "isn't it always so *cold*" responses when the subject comes up at dinner parties. Good ski clothing should keep you warm and dry, but should also allow a maximum freedom of movement and provide for good ventilation during aerobic activity. See a good outfitter for technical advice on the latest in ski clothing technology.

Cotton is the worst of all fibers for ski touring because it readily absorbs moisture, conducts heat away from the body, and takes a very long time to dry. A number of new high-tech synthetic fabrics, or simply old-fashioned wool, are much better. Merino wool is particularly comfortable, very durable, and reduces the problem of itchiness often associated with ordinary wool. Layered clothing is far superior to a single cumbersome parka and thick "ski bibs," which are generally too warm to wear while skiing and seriously restrict maneuverability. You will want to dress particularly light during aerobic uphill skiing, but you should carry additional layers to add when it gets cold, rains, snows, or you settle down for a lunch break after sweating it up the hill. Gaiters are also an essential item in backcountry conditions to keep snow from entering through the tops of the boots.

Extra clothing. Several thin layers are always better than one humongous parka. Although you will keep warm through physical activity while skiing, the body will cool off very quickly when stopped. Bring an extra warm sweater, wool hat, and mittens for when you stop to rest or eat. These should fit over your lighter-weight skiing clothes, which should, of course, be of suitable fabric.

Food and water, and extra food and water. Bring enough food and water for lunch (and then some) if you'll be out for a full day. But also bring on-the-trail snacks and emergency high-energy items such as high-calorie energy bars. Insulated or vacuum-flask bottles may be necessary in extremely cold and overnight conditions.

Sunglasses, sunscreen, and sunscreen lip-balm. Use sunscreen and sunscreen lip-balm before it becomes very sunny, and re-apply frequently throughout the day. Even if there is thick cloud cover, you will still soak up the harmful UV-rays, especially during spring and at higher elevations. Sunglasses will not only make skiing more pleasant, they will protect your eyes from the damaging rays, and possibly from snow blindness in extreme conditions. Be sure that the lenses have a full UV-filter.

Pocket knife or other multi-tool. This kit should at least include a knife for cutting rope and a set of screwdrivers and pliers for other repairs. Those with small saw blades are often handy.

First-aid emergency kit. The minimum kit should include, but is not limited to, the following: adhesive tape, gauze and bandages, moleskin (for blisters; 5 by 5 inches or larger), pain killers and muscle relaxants, emergency blanket, and antiseptic. Other suggested items, based on special needs and the length of the ski tour, include first-aid manual, hand-warmers, thermometer, tweezers, needle and thread, safety gloves, scissors, medical tape, wire splint, additional bandages (compress, butterfly, triangular, etc.), burn ointment, and cough drops, among other specialty items. A mobile phone is particularly useful in case of emergency, although loose change or a calling card may be necessary in areas with poor network coverage.

Don't forget toilet paper (in a waterproof plastic bag). Truly hard-core appreciators of the backcountry will also bring two-layered plastic bags for carrying out.

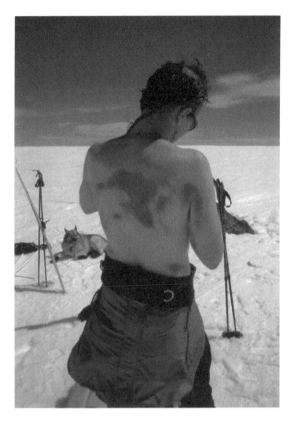

Oregon boy goes to the desert. Apply sunscreen evenly and thoroughly!

Fire starting materials. These should include waterproof matches, a plumber's candle (available at hardware stores), and fire-starter fuel. Winter is a difficult time to get an emergency fire started, and matches alone will *not* suffice. The plumber's candle is particularly useful for drying out fuel when matches alone just won't start a fire.

Flashlight. Your flashlight should be a small model, with new/extra batteries and extra bulb. The "headlamp" variety is particularly useful for emergency or planned after-dark skiing (moonlight and starlight tours).

Map. For many of the beginner tours, which travel along marked winter routes, the maps provided here will suffice. However, for backcountry skiing, especially away from the marked route, the appropriate USGS quadrangles will be particularly useful navigation tools.

Compass (and GPS if available). Know how to use these instruments, in conjunction with the appropriate maps, *before* going out into the backcountry.

Repair kit. This should include *duct tape* (which fixes almost anything!), small screwdrivers, and replacement screws (for binding and other repairs), extra pole basket, and nylon rope (another all-purpose fix-it). One idea is to wrap a good length of duct tape around your pole, and keep it there for emergency use (it remains sticky). Other suggestions, depending on your handiness and the length of the ski tour, include epoxy, pole splint, ski splint, baling wire, and additional spare parts.

Waxing gear (if using waxable skis). Ski touring in southern Utah requires a wide range of grip wax and klister temperatures for changing conditions, as well as a cork for smoothing, and a scraper for removal of old wax. Extra wipe-on glide wax is often useful for both waxless and waxable skis in abrasive snow conditions.

Nordic Ski Waxing

Ski waxing is a subject requiring a book of its own. Although most skiers these days use waxless skis, the subject of waxing skis for grip in southern Utah weather requires some discussion for the few hard-cores who still practice the "ancient art" of ski waxing. Even in good waxing conditions, waxable skis can be frustrating for the inexperienced. In many cases, the snow conditions of southern Utah are less than ideal for waxable skis, even for the experienced ski waxer. However, when the wax used meets the snow conditions just right, the feeling of a perfect grip during kick and a long smooth glide simply cannot be beat. Waxable skis, when waxed correctly, can improve overall speed dramatically, leaving you to work much less than any companions on the waxless variety, and to pass them on both the uphills and the downhills, as well as on the flats in between.

For those who are unfamiliar with waxing techniques, there are entire books and often weekly clinics devoted to the subject. Every experienced ski waxer has his own "special brew" of waxing products. This book cannot go into the details of waxing in total, but can provide some guidance for the unique weather and snow conditions of southern Utah that affect ski waxing. Following are a few hints.

Warm waxes. Southern Utah is nothing like Minnesota, Norway, or Fairbanks, Alaska. The temperature is generally warm, except when an occasional cold front blows through. Even during winter storms, daytime temperature rarely falls below 10°F (−12°C). Because of the relatively dry climate, temperatures change rapidly throughout the day, and often hover around the critical value of freezing. Although a base layer of green wax often helps to retain additional warmer wax layers, purples, reds, and klisters often get the most usage in this country.

At-home waxing. Don't wax at home. It may seem convenient to wax in the warmth and comfort of your living room, but you have no idea what the temperature will be on the trail, even if you've looked at the local forecast. In the end, you will find yourself adding or subtracting wax layers at the trailhead if you succumb to this folly.

Changing conditions. The temperatures of southern Utah are changing constantly with cloud cover, time of day, and fast-moving storm tracks. Consequently, you may need to add a layer of warmer wax at midday, or scrape off the layer of warm wax toward sunset. Be prepared with a wide variety of wax temperatures, and with the necessary tools. Keep these in a handy position like a jacket pocket, instead of in your pack below your lunch.

Klister. Klister is a real necessity. Although the mountains of southern Utah do get large quantities of snow annually, storm events are relatively infrequent, and conditions can become icy and abrasive on waxes due to widely variable daily temperatures and to extended dry periods between storms. These sorts of conditions require the use of klister waxes, which are designed for old and abrasive snow.

Layering/mixing waxes and klister. One of the best techniques for the variable conditions of southern Utah is to use a mix of a variety of waxes and/or klister, making a composite wax zone that will adapt well to all types of conditions to be experienced throughout the day. Apply a layer of cool-temperature wax/klister on the base to stop warmer layers from being removed by abrasion. It is often useful to iron in a layer of green or base wax as a preparation for layers of warmer wax. Add layers of wax in thin successional layers from cool greens and blues to the warmest color needed. This also allows the ski to stick in cooler spots, such as shaded areas, while still gripping with the warmer wax in sunnier snow.

Icing up. This can be the greatest nuisance to the waxing skier, and it is a very common problem in the rapidly changing conditions of southern Utah. When snow conditions are too cold or fresh for the wax used, large clumps of snow will adhere permanently to the grip zone of the ski. To avoid this nuisance, use cooler waxes at first, and add warmer colors as necessary. If needed, simply scrape off the offending warm wax. Sometimes simply removing the iced-up snow with a hand or scraper will temporarily remedy the condition. At other times, sliding the ski quickly under foot in place will remove the clumps.

Ski Techniques

Most of the ski and snowshoe routes described in this book are in no way properly groomed, and many are wholly untracked. Consequently, the style of skiing appropriate for southern Utah is different from that for the larger cross-country resorts and trails of the U.S. east coast or the upper Midwest, or much of Europe. Although groomed trails, with tracks set for both classical and freestyle skiing, can be found at Ruby's Inn at Bryce Canyon and Brian Head Ski Resort (see Ski Touring Areas 1 and 2), resort-quality groomed trails are relatively rare among the many backcountry routes and tracks. Even among these backcountry trails, only the most frequently used ski routes are marked for winter touring (with the standard "blue diamonds" set by the Forest Service). Most tours described in this book are true backcountry routes, following snowed-over summer roads and hiking trails, and are entirely lacking winter trail markings. Cross-country skiing on these types of trails requires the use of additional skills beyond the common diagonal stride or skating methods. On steep narrow trails, skills in herringboning or side-stepping are frequently required. Additional downhill techniques, such as more advanced turning techniques, may be necessary for some of the hairier descents in the more advanced areas outside the scope of this book. However, all of the terrain described in this book is relatively gentle, so familiarity with extreme downhill and advanced turning techniques is not necessary. If unfamiliar with this type of skiing, which I'd think of as "classical backcountry ski touring," the reader is referred to several more extensive books on backcountry skiing for a more thorough discussion of backcountry tips and techniques (see Recommended Reading at the back of this book). Ski lessons, available through many retail shops and ski clubs, are also a good way to pick up on techniques appropriate for the terrain.

Weather

Conditions in southern Utah can change quickly and dramatically. Furthermore, weather forecasts for the area are generally vague, and are intended for the more inhabited valleys such as Cedar City and St. George. The conditions on the mountain are entirely different from the forecast locations, generally colder by 20–30°F, and much different in terms of cloud cover. Plan and prepare for the worst possible conditions first by bringing all potentially necessary gear with you, and second by carrying the gear you will need in your pack. You will more likely regret not having that extra sweater when it gets cold than you will regret having to carry it on the trail if it stays warm.

Avalanches

Avalanche rescue techniques are a subject of their own and beyond the scope of this book, which provides only an outline of the basic premises of avalanche avoidance. Avalanche danger is generally mild in most of the southern Utah plateau country, but it can be significant in some of the backcountry areas described in this book, and outside the boundaries of ski resorts. If you are traveling into areas where avalanche danger is notable (avalanche-prone areas are noted in this book, but include many areas outside the described trails), make sure that you are very familiar with avalanche techniques and equipment. Entire short courses, seminars, and books are dedicated to the subject, so unfamiliarity with this danger is no excuse. The best way to avoid being trapped in an avalanche is to simply not ski in avalanche-prone areas. However, all skiers should be familiar with a few basic techniques for avoiding and surviving an avalanche:

- Do not ski under cornices, on steep slopes with fresh snow, narrow canyons with steep walls, or areas of known previous avalanches.
- If your party is crossing a potential avalanche surface, ski across one at a time, so as to apply minimum pressure to the potential failure surface, and to have other party members available for a possible rescue.
- If you are caught in an avalanche, stay calm, and try to float to the top and side of the flow using swimming motions (the "breaststroke" is best). Do not fight the flow, but go with it, and maintain the optimum position for survival once the avalanche has stopped.
- Just before the avalanche comes to a stop, try to make an air pocket available for breathing while you wait for rescue.
- Ski with others in avalanche country, because if one member of the party is caught, that person's only hope is a rescue by others. To find an avalanche victim, keep your eye on him or his gear during the avalanche runout. As soon as the avalanche stops, all other members of the party should begin probing the area immediately below the point where the victim was last seen.
- If you spend a lot of time skiing in avalanche country, be equipped with rescue equipment such as beacons and probing poles. Also be very familiar with how to use this equipment before you have to use it.

Other Hazards

Cross-country skiing and snowshoeing, when done properly, are generally low-risk activities. However, familiarity with the terrain is essential. Much of the high plateau skiing is best experienced from the rim of steep escarpments, the margins of which can be slippery when covered in snow and ice. Tree wells (depressions left by a lack of snow below trees) can become very deep in spring, and must be avoided when one is skiing through forested areas. Tree branches, rocks, and other hazards do exist, making a familiarity with basic first-aid practices essential.

Winter First Aid

Hypothermia and frostbite are two potential conditions to add to normal outdoor first-aid precautions while ski touring. Hypothermia is caused by exposure to cold temperatures, but it is exacerbated by wet clothes, wind, and exhaustion. Uncontrollable shivering is the first sign of hypothermia, and is followed by worsening symptoms affecting the nervous system, such as slurred speech, incoherence, memory lapse, drowsiness, clumsiness, exhaustion, and loss of motor control of the hands. These final signs may not be recognized by the victim, so be aware of your touring partners' conditions and of the symptoms of hypothermia.

To avoid hypothermia, avoid excessive sweating by wearing proper clothing (layering), carrying proper additional clothing, eating often, and eating high-energy foods. To treat hypothermia, first get the victim to shelter, and then add heat: apply extra layers of clothing, give warm liquids, apply a warm water bottle to the skin, build a fire, and give quick-energy foods. Do not give the victim alcohol. Skin-to-skin contact will heat much more quickly than putting the victim in a sleeping bag alone. Do not put the victim to sleep. Keep the victim active, but do not overexert.

Frostbite is the actual freezing of the liquid in body parts, and is less of a danger in southern Utah than in many other places of more extreme temperatures. However, if you have ever experienced loss of sensation in the extremities (fingers, toes, ears, noses, and cheeks are most susceptible), coupled with a white or gray appearance of the tissue, this is probably the onset of frostbite. To treat frostbite, warm the affected skin immediately, preferably by skin-to-skin contact with warm parts of the body (the stomach area is a particularly good heat source). If possible, apply a warm water bottle or heat pack to the affected areas. Do *not* rub, vibrate, or disturb the frozen skin tissue, as this will cause further damage. Do not simply add extra socks to cold toes in boots, as this will reduce the warming of blood supply to the affected area.

Trail Etiquette

One of the purposes of this book is to expand the winter touring possibilities in southern Utah for the rapidly growing sports of ski touring and snowshoeing in order to disperse the growing number of tourers in such a way as to minimize human impact on the landscape and personal experiences. As the number of winter tourers grows nationally, and particularly in southern Utah, there will become an increasing need for "getting along well with others." Following are a few guidelines for minimizing your effects on the backcountry experience of others, as well as the human effects on the landscape.

- Allow faster skiers to pass, especially on downhills. When you stop to take even a brief rest, step off to the side of the track, so that others may ski through. Uphill skiers should yield the track to an approaching downhill skier by stepping out of the track until the skier passes.
- If you are breaking trail through the backcountry, set a good, straight track with consideration for skiers who will follow, as well as for your return trip. If you are following an already set track, improve it. A well-set track can make skiing a pleasure. Following sets of wandering tracks with wavering distances between skis can make an experience miserable.
- Do not walk or snowshoe on established ski tracks. Most winter walkers and snowshoers do not know what kind of pet-peeve this is among ski tourers. The post-holes made by hiking boots or the miniature moguls made by snowshoers can make skiing not only unpleasant, but also very difficult. These ski tracks help maintain direction while skiing. Similarly, snowmobilers should avoid running over established ski tracks. (Note that the converse does not apply—snowmobilers do not seem to mind that skiers follow over their tracks).
- If you ski with a dog, either ski in areas where dogs are allowed and common, or ski where there are no other skiers. Although they make the best ski companions, dogs, like snowshoers and walkers, can ruin a great set of ski tracks with their own little footprints. Dog-skiers should also clean up after their companions. If you can, find a way to ski with your dog attached (like skijoring), so that your friend does not interfere with other skiers.
- Fill in the depressions left by falls (sitzmarks). These can become giant holes to skiers following your tracks. After replacing the snow, reestablish a track by skiing over the sitzmark.
- When skiing on or near downhill resorts, either avoid ski runs or

stay at their margins. If you must cross a ski run, do not interfere with the traffic, and do so quickly.
- Respect the private property of others. Consider the rights of property owners and other drivers when looking for parking at or near trailheads.
- Pack out any litter. This includes small candy wrappers, toilet paper, and even cigarette butts. Follow the old adage, "If you pack it in, pack it out."

Snowmobiles

Skiers generally have one of several attitudes toward snowmobiles, ranging from complete despisal, through acceptance, even to appreciation. It's true that the sight, sound, smell, and even taste of snowmobiles can ruin an otherwise perfect backcountry experience. The noise of the typical two-stroke engines can be heard like giant mosquitoes from many miles away. The smell of the exhaust-particle-laden fumes is noxious to skiers and snowshoers, who are accustomed to the pleasure of breathing in clean, crisp winter air. The taste of snowmobile engine fumes can linger in the air for several minutes after one of the less-well-tuned machines has passed. Furthermore, heavily tracked shared-use trails become icy and difficult to navigate on skis. And sometimes you just want to know that when you're out in the backcountry, the only creatures around you got there on muscle power alone.

All this having been said, in some cases shared-use trails can have their advantages. When the snowmobiles themselves have passed by, a single machine or small group in single file can leave behind a well-compacted but not icy trail that, if not overused, can significantly minimize the difficulties of trailbreaking. When at all possible, muscle-powered winter tourers should seek to find ways to get along with the ever-present snowmobilers and encourage the benefits of "shared use." Few of the trails in southern Utah are reserved and designated for muscle-powered touring alone, so skiers and snowshoers must at least make an effort to find a way of coexisting with snowmobilers. This can be done first by being friendly with snowmobilers (they are generally very nice people), and then by talking with them and educating them as to the particular needs of skiers and snowshoers on shared-use trails.

Access to Trailheads

Because of the slim populations of skiers in southern Utah, parking opportunities at trailheads are relatively few. In the case of many of the trails described here, there is little to no organized parking for winter ski and snowshoe tourers. This means that special attention needs to be paid in making plans for transportation and parking. Use as few vehicles as possible (carpool), and consider others (both other skiers and drivers) when finding a place for your four-wheeled transportation. If you need to pull off to the side of the road, do so in a safe location that does not inhibit traffic. Do not park in private driveways, even if they appear to lead to summer homes that are abandoned for the winter season. Special attention should be paid to property ownership rights and changes in development around the rapidly growing Brian Head and Elk Meadows ski areas. The spot you parked your car in last year may now be somebody's driveway. Check with local authorities in these areas if parking and road conditions seem to have changed from the time the descriptions here were made. Skier consciousness of these delicate matters will assure the future of cross-country skiing in southern Utah, by establishing good relationships with local authorities and land owners.

4. How to Use this Book

Each of the following five sections describes a number of beginner to advanced ski and snowshoe touring routes, the major features of which are summarized in a table in the area introduction. For those who use GPS systems, a table of coordinates for all of the trailheads can be found in the appendix at the back of this book. Each trail is given a designation of trail difficulty using one of the following broadly defined categories.

Beginner

Beginner trails are intended for first-time and novice skiers. These routes are short (typically less than three miles round trip), and can be skied at the slow, learning pace of novices, within a casual-paced morning or afternoon. These trails are also characterized by very gentle terrain (less than a few hundred feet elevation gain and loss), making the routes much less strenuous and easier to ski with a less advanced set of skiing and backcountry skills. These trails require little skill in terms of striding techniques, turning, stopping, or control on downhills. These trails are also well marked and require no route-finding skills unless specified.

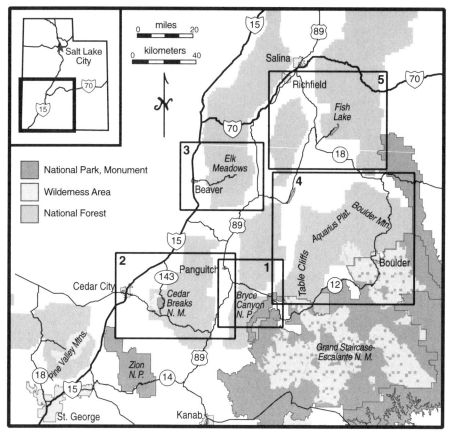

Ski Touring Areas:
1. Paunsagunt Plateau (including Bryce Canyon National Park).
2. Markagunt Plateau (including Cedar Breaks National Monument, Brian Head Ski Resort).
3. Tushar Mountains (including Elk Meadows Ski Resort).
4. Aquarius, Boulder and Table Cliffs Plateaus.
5. Fish Lake Plateau.

Intermediate

Trails identified as "intermediate" are meant for skiers and snowshoers of moderate experience and ability. These trails have some challenging terrain, with occasional steep or woodsy sections. Elevation gain and total distance are also more substantial. These trails sometimes require additional route-finding skills, as they are generally unmarked or marked only for summer travel. Intermediate skiers should be comfortable with using a map, compass, and/or GPS to navigate longer routes (up to seven miles round trip), and should be prepared with the additional backcountry equipment and skills necessary for these more distant ventures from civilization.

Advanced

These routes are intended only for seasoned and well-prepared skiers and snowshoers. Advanced routes require mastery of all skiing skills and cover the steepest of terrain found in the area. Skiers should be comfortable with downhill skiing techniques (on skinny skis), and be able to ski in control on all types of terrain. Advanced skiers should be fully equipped to account for their own safety and comfort in all types of conditions. Advanced routes are long (typically greater than ten miles round trip), and require the strength and stamina to ski all day long. Although all of the routes described in this book can be skied within a short winter's day, many of the long-distance backcountry routes may be done as winter overnight or longer trips—especially with additional mileage into the deeper backcountry.

Backcountry

The term "backcountry" is used in this book to describe unmarked and often untracked trails, and is therefore applied to routes of all difficulty levels, but more often to intermediate and advanced routes. Although most of the backcountry trails fit into the advanced and intermediate levels described above, there are a few beginner tours, that is, tours of short distance and gentle terrain, that follow backcountry routes. Although the beginner backcountry tours require minimal skiing skills, all backcountry skiers should be prepared with the appropriate route-finding skills and equipment, even on the shortest beginner routes. The beginner backcountry routes should be attempted only by first-time skiers who are otherwise comfortable with standard techniques required for backcountry travel. The more advanced backcountry routes (intermediate to advanced categories) traverse steeper terrain, and should be attempted only by those properly equipped for repairs, avalanches, or other emergencies.

Although maps are provided for each of the tours described here, skiers—especially advanced and backcountry skiers—should build up a library of the appropriate 7.5-minute quadrangle maps available from the U.S. Geological Survey. These will be essential tools (along with a compass and GPS system) for finding the trails and routes described, and particularly for going beyond the described areas.

The Ski Tours

AREA 1

Bryce Canyon and Surroundings, Including Ruby's Inn Resort
Eocene Lakes of the Paunsagunt Plateau

Bryce Canyon National Park, situated on the rim of the Paunsagunt Plateau, is truly the crown jewel of ski touring in southwestern Utah. Not only is the scenery sensational, but the winter services and facilities provided by Ruby's Inn and the National Park Service make for perfect weekend ski getaways. Just outside the park boundaries, Ruby's Inn grooms dozens of kilometers of trail for both classical and freestyle skiing. Within the park, the National Park Service marks winter trails and sets classical tracks on several additional backcountry routes. Beyond the groomed and marked system of trails near the park entrance, a wide variety of scarcely traveled backcountry routes can be found throughout the entire Paunsagunt Plateau area.

The scenery at Bryce during winter is unsurpassed, and is known best for its combination of red rocks, blue sky, and white snow. All along the plateau escarpment, the Paunsagunt Fault system exposes the chromic outcrops of the Pink Cliffs, composed of the Eocene Claron Formation (see geological history below). The 1,000-ft. (310-m.) rock exposures in the canyon walls and amphitheaters present the brightly colored rocks in magnificent arrays of hoodoos, goblins, and a variety of odd and indescribable landforms. The air at Bryce Canyon is much cleaner during the winter lull in tourist activity, so visibility is at a maximum (as much as 110 mi. or 183 km., compared to 85 mi. or 140 km. during the summer tourist boom). Even in winter, most days are clear, with the unadulterated deep blue of winter skies at a maximum. With luck, skiers will find that fresh dustings of snow have fallen during the evenings, leaving a surface of pure white joy. Besides the exotic geological scenery at the rim of Bryce Canyon, the ramping surface of the Paunsagunt Plateau is characterized by the unique charm of Ponderosa pine (*Pinus ponderosa*) forests, whose characteristic open forested conditions provide ideal terrain for ski touring and snowshoeing. These plateaus are sometimes covered with dense patches of Greenleaf manzanita (*Arctostaphylos patula*), which can sometimes be caught under skis. At some of the higher elevations within the park, one may see a few examples of the contorted Bristlecone pine (*Pinus longaeva*), which are frequently characteristic of the rim exposures of the Pink Cliffs.

Ruby's Inn, conveniently located at the entrance to Bryce Canyon National Park, offers discounted winter room rates, restaurants, supplies, shopping, hot tubs, a swimming pool, and many other facilities to make for a perfect winter touring destination. The number of tourists at Bryce in winter is nowhere near comparable to the summer boom, when hundreds of tour buses and thousands of visitors cycle through the park every day. Although the Park Service does see enough traffic to keep its facilities operational during winter, crowds are minimal. Fortunately for skiers, the Park Service also attempts to keep the Bryce Canyon road to the end of the park (Highway 63) open during most weather and winter driving conditions, providing access to the ski terrain within the park.

Over Presidents' Day weekend (in mid to late February), Ruby's Inn hosts the annual Winter Festival at Bryce Canyon, in cooperation with the National Park Service and a number of organizations and retailers based in Salt Lake City. During this weekend ski extravaganza, a few hundred skiers flock to the resort at the park entrance and participate in activities such as organized ski races, ski and snowshoe tours, demonstrations, photo competitions, and an all-around good time. It is a good chance to get to know other skiers who enjoy the red rock country, and to find and ski new winter tours.

Geology of Bryce Canyon National Park

The term "canyon," applied to the Bryce "Canyon" escarpment by early settlers, is something of a misnomer, in that there is no gorge through which a stream flows. Rather, this landscape, and the boundaries of the Bryce Canyon National Park, encompass the elongate north-south-trending escarpment of the Paunsagunt Plateau. The rim of the escarpment provides extended views into several expansive amphitheaters, to small mesas and promontories, the whole of which is

Racer in the Bryce Canyon/Ruby's Inn Winter Festival 10k race

studded with variously shaped rock chimneys, or "hoodoos." These erosional landscape features elude description and lack specific geological names, but have been variously called "hoodoos," "spires," "pedestals," "fins," "pinnacles," "goblins," "temples," and "castles," among probably many other creative names. However, there really exists no way to describe this unique landscape without a photograph. The red, pink, lavender, orange, and white rocks exposed in the cliffs of Bryce Canyon belong to the Eocene Claron Formation, which is the same rock unit found at Cedar Breaks National Monument and in the Pink Cliffs near Cedar City, as well as in the wall of the high Table Cliffs Plateau, the prominent cliffs visible in the distance from the rim at Bryce. During the Cenozoic Era (65 million years ago to the present), these rocks were deposited by a continuous depositional system of lakes and rivers.

The lower 700 ft. (220 m.) of the rocks that belong to the Claron Formation, including the bright red and pink rocks that give Bryce its chroma, were deposited by a system of rivers and deltas in a gently subsiding and flat basin. This river system is evidenced by the repeating fining-upwards cycles of deposition, which are characteristic of this depositional environment. These cycles, each a few meters thick, begin at their base with a sharp transition to coarse gravel or sand and gradually become finer in particle size upwards, eventually being composed of silt and finer clay particles near the top.

It is the very nature of these fining-upwards cycles that gives the hoodoos of Bryce their form and shapeliness. The clayey deposits at the tops of the cycles are more susceptible to erosion than the sandier deposits, and make the narrow "necks" to some of the pinnacles. At the base of the fining-upwards cycles, the abrupt transition to coarse sandy deposits, which are less susceptible to erosion and therefore wider in profile view, produces the "balancing rocks," such as Thor's Hammer, which can be seen from Inspiration Point (see Ski Tour 4). Throughout the Bryce Canyon exposures, this cyclicity of fining-upwards sequences is evident. The curvy shapes of the exposures are the result of differential erosion of these regular cycles of more erodable claystone (indentations in profile view), alternating with more resistant sandstone (bulges in profile view).

This texture of the erosional landscape is also played upon by slight color differences between each of these types of geological deposits. The sandstones are more quartz-rich (because quartz is most commonly found as sand-sized particles), making the sandstones somewhat subdued in their shade of color, lighter and more subtle. The claystones contain more abundant oxidized iron minerals, most commonly found as clay-sized particles, giving these layers increasingly intense red, pink, orange, and yellow hues.

The difference in the intensity of color in these alternating cycles is related to the different environments of deposition in which the sandstone and mudstone deposits formed. The mudstones (composed of finer clay and silt particles) are deposits of rivers on their floodplains, where murky pools deposit thin layers of mud following seasonal floods.

However, these floodplain deposits are also overprinted with fossil soils, or paleosols. These paleosols are evidence of long periods of exposure of the ancient landscape to the processes of soil formation, in between the relatively infrequent intervals of deposition by flooding events. It was the highly oxidizing conditions of these ancient soil environments that gave the cliffs of the Paunsagunt Plateau their bright red colors, now characterized by the iron mineral hematite, known by its rusty color. The sandstone deposits, on the other hand, were deposited by the waters of fast-moving rivers, which sorted out most of the finer clays and silts, leaving behind the less colorful sand-sized grains of quartz, and a few other similar minerals.

The upper 300 ft. (90 m.) of the Claron Formation, including the predominantly white- to buff-colored rocks seen capping the plateau south of Sunrise Point, consist of limestones deposited by a very large shallow lake or system of shallow lakes that existed in a much flatter southern Utah during the Eocene period. These lakes are evidenced by

Snow drifts on the Claron Formation

the nature of the rocks themselves, as well as a few freshwater snails and clams found within. The ancient environment of these lakes can be compared to similar lakes of the Bolivian and Peruvian Altiplano, a high plateau country in the lee of the Andes Mountains, with large shallow lakes that are currently depositing limestones with features similar to those of the Claron Formation.

Despite this curious geological history of deposition and soil formation, the exotic textures of the amphitheaters at Bryce Canyon are less related to the geological composition of the strata exposed than to their more recent erosion. Since formation of the lake and paleosol deposits, the rocks have been buried under kilometers of volcanic debris (see geological history of the Tushar Range in Ski Touring Area 3), only to be re-exposed during the more recent uplift of the high plateaus region. This uplift has caused the crust to break along a number of major faults, some of which are currently active (see geological history in Ski Touring Area 2). One of these, the Paunsagunt Fault, traverses the base of the cliffs of the Paunsagunt Plateau and has upthrown the eastern block, leaving the underlying marine shales of the Tropic Valley very susceptible to erosion, and thereby causing cliff retreat of the more resistant rocks on the Paunsagunt Rim. These erosional processes have been exacerbated by the downcutting of the Colorado River system, which in turn has been caused by major tectonic forces involved in the

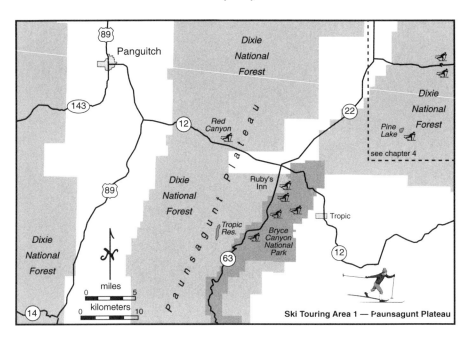

Ski Touring Area 1 — Paunsagunt Plateau

Area 1 Ski Tours

Map No.	Ski Tour	Length in mi. (km.)*	Difficulty and Notes*
Ruby's Inn Area			
1	To the Rim and Back	1.7 mi. (2.9 km.) RT	B (S)
2	Forest Loop	4.0 mi. (6.6 km.) LP	I (BC)
3	Bryce Town Loop	3.1 mi. (5.1 km.) LP	B
Bryce Canyon Area			
4	Inspiration–Bryce Points	2.7 mi. (4.5 km.) RT	I (BC, S)
5	Paria Loop	3.1 mi. (5.2 km.) LP	B (BC, S)
6	Sunset to Tropic	2.5 mi. (4.2 km.) OW	I (BC, S)
7	Sunset Loop	5.8 mi. (9.6 km.) LP	I (BC, S)
8	Paria View–Bryce Loop	2.7 mi. (4.5 km.) LP	I (BC, S)
Other Areas			
9	Casto Canyon	4.2 mi. (7.0 km.) RT	I (BC, S)

*RT = Round trip; OW = One way; LP = Loop; B = Beginner; I = Intermediate; BC = Backcountry route, unmarked trail; S = Also recommended for snowshoes.

opening of the Gulf of California. The activity of this faulting and downcutting is relatively recent in geological terms, and is the reason for the geologically unstable slopes of the high Paunsagunt escarpment. It has been estimated that this slope retreats at an average rate of 4 ft. (1.2 m.) per century. Continuing at this rate, the entire plateau will have been eroded in a little over a million years.

Tour 1: To the Rim and Back

Tour Length: 1.7 mi. (2.9 km.) round trip.

Difficulty: Very easy beginner route. The trail is very flat and regularly groomed. It is a very easy way for first-time and beginning skiers to access the views from the plateau rim outside the national park. This is also a very easy snowshoe tour, and makes for good moonlight and starlight tours.

Elevation: 7,660–7,700 ft. (2,330–2,340 m.).

Snow Conditions: Generally skiable from December through March, although snow conditions are highly variable annually. February and

Skiing the rim at Bryce Canyon, Boat Mesa in the background

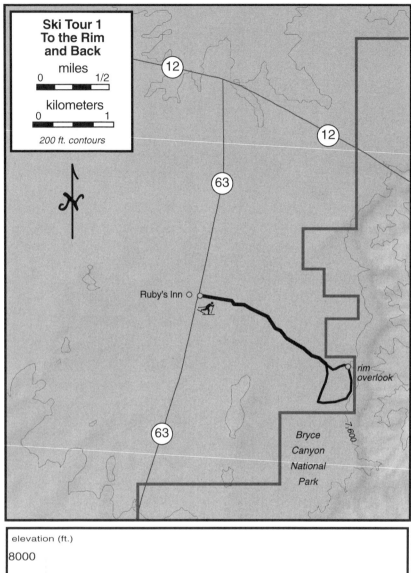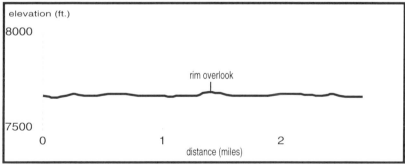

March are generally the best months for deepest snow cover. This route is part of the Ruby's Inn/Bryce Canyon groomed track system, which is set for both freestyle and classical skiing. Snowshoers should walk outside of the groomed areas.

Geological and Other Scenic Features: A nice view of the exposures of the Claron Formation from an unnamed viewpoint at the rim of the Paunsagunt Plateau.

Other Useful Maps: National Park Service Map "Bryce Canyon National Park," Trails Illustrated Map "Bryce Canyon National Park," and U.S. Geological Survey 7.5-minute Quadrangle "Bryce Canyon."

How to Get There (Paunsagunt Plateau Area Map)

This tour is accessible from the Ruby's Inn Center and trailhead. To get to Ruby's Inn, take Highway 12 from Highway 89 near Panguitch for 13 mi. to the intersection with Highway 63. Turn right on Highway 63 toward Bryce Canyon National Park. Ruby's Inn is about 1 mi. south of the intersection and 2 mi. north of the entrance to Bryce Canyon National Park. Park at the main entrance to the inn and walk across the street to the trailhead.

Ski Tour Description

If you do one simple ski or snowshoe tour while at Bryce Canyon, this should be it. It is an easy stroll out to the rim, and the trail follows nicely groomed routes without the interference of snowmobiles. This trail is generally very good for track skiers accustomed to neatly groomed trails. The Rim Trail is also an easy way to access the many other kilometers of trail that are regularly groomed by Ruby's Inn and marked and set by the National Park Service. For a unique experience, this tour makes for an excellent moonlight tour, or even a starlight tour, depending on the lunar cycle. If you do this, be sure to be careful near the plateau edge, and to bring adequate lighting (especially if traveling by starlight). A headlamp is ideal for hands-free use while skiing. Although this is an easy snowshoe tour, avoid the temptation to walk on the groomed tracks.

From the parking area at Ruby's Inn, cross the highway toward the small, rustic-looking shops out in front (which are closed in winter). Just to the left (north) of these buildings, the trailhead begins. Follow the groomed tracks up a gentle incline, traveling nearly due west. The trail enters the forest for a short while and emerges as soon as it begins to descend the final gentle incline to the rim. From the rim, you can take a short loop that follows along the edge and quickly returns to the original route, which can then be followed back to the parking area. This route also intersects some of the other Ruby's Inn groomed routes such as the Forest Loop (see Ski Tour 2), and Bryce Town Loop (see Ski Tour 3).

Tour 2: Forest Loop

Tour Length: 4.0 mi. (6.6 km.) loop.

Difficulty: Easier intermediate route. Much of this trail is very flat and regularly groomed. However, at the rim this trail leaves the groomed system and follows an easy backcountry route through the forests within the national park. The route is marked by the Park Service, and most often is well tracked and easy to follow. There is also a substantial elevation gain in climbing along the plateau edge.

Elevation: 7,660–7,840 ft. (2,330–2,420 m.).

Snow Conditions: Generally skiable from December through March. Snow conditions are highly variable annually. The best snow is generally in February to March. The beginning of this route follows the Ruby's Inn/Bryce Canyon groomed track, where packing retains snow well. This section is followed by a backcountry tour through the forest, where snow may occasionally be spotty and/or crusty.

Geological and Other Scenic Features: A nice view from the rim at an unnamed viewpoint at the rim of the Paunsagunt Plateau, followed by tours through the open Ponderosa pine forests on the plateau surface.

Other Useful Maps: National Park Service Map "Bryce Canyon National Park," Trails Illustrated Map "Bryce Canyon National Park," and U.S. Geological Survey 7.5-minute Quadrangle "Bryce Canyon."

How to Get There (Paunsagunt Plateau Area Map)

This trail is accessible from the Ruby's Inn Center and trailhead. See directions for Ski Tour 1—To the Rim and Back.

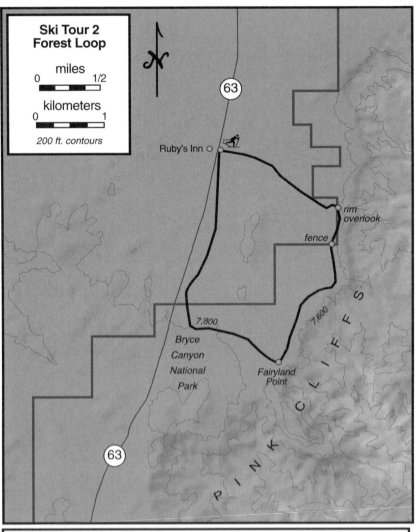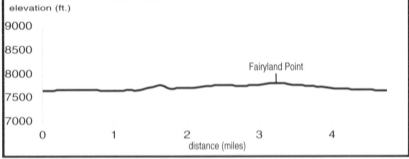

Ski Tour Description

This tour travels along the Paunsagunt rim escarpment for a considerable distance, and then continues through some of the forests and meadows typical of the high plateaus of southern Utah. It is an excellent addition to the short trip to the rim (see Ski Tour 1), and easily skiable if you have a bit of extra ski time.

From the trailhead area, follow the Rim Trail to the viewpoint at the plateau edge (see Ski Tour 1). Continue south along the rim about 0.2 mi. (0.3 km.) to the boundary of the National Park. At about this point, the groomed Rim Trail (Ski Tour 1) loops back to the east, while the Forest Loop (this tour) continues south along a marked and well-skied backcountry trail. The continuation of this trail is marked by a wire fence with an opening for skiers to continue farther southward along the rim. Continue to ski along the rim, with several viewpoints to a marked signpost for the Forest Loop return route. The trail returns through the forest, to the Fairyland Point Trailhead and parking area on Highway 63. One can either leave a car at this area, hitchhike back to Ruby's Inn, or ski alongside the road to return to the trailhead at Ruby's. Note that that the Park Service charges entrance fees to the park, so be prepared to pay if you choose to leave a car at the Fairyland Point Trailhead.

Tour 3: Bryce Town Loop

Tour Length: 3.1 mi. (5.1 km.) loop.

Difficulty: More difficult beginner route. This trail is regularly groomed, and much of it is generally flat. About halfway through the tour there is a substantial elevation gain, which climbs over an oblong hill on the plateau surface, providing something of a workout for track skiers.

Elevation: 7,660–7,820 ft. (2,330–2,410 m.).

Snow Conditions: Generally skiable from December through March, although snow conditions are highly variable annually. Snow is usually at its best in February and March. This route is part of the Ruby's Inn/Bryce Canyon groomed track, which is set for both freestyle and classical skiing.

Geological and Other Scenic Features: Gentle tours through the open Ponderosa pine forests of the Paunsagunt Plateau.

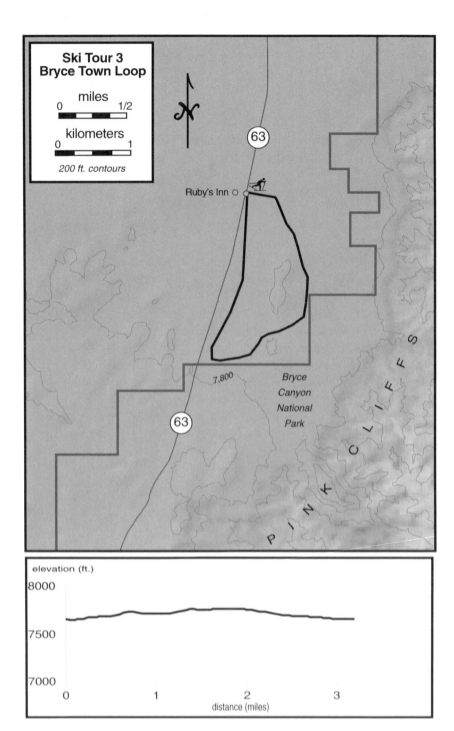

Other Useful Maps: National Park Service Map "Bryce Canyon National Park," Trails Illustrated Map "Bryce Canyon National Park," and U.S. Geological Survey 7.5-minute Quadrangle "Bryce Canyon."

How to Get There (Paunsagunt Plateau Area Map)

This tour is accessible from the Ruby's Inn Center. See directions for Ski Tour 1—To the Rim and Back.

Ski Tour Description

This tour can be done by itself, but it is also a great add-on to the short trip to the rim and back (Ski Tour 1). For track skiers it makes a great training loop, with a substantial hill climb at the center. For beginning skiers it is a great way to experience the open Ponderosa forests typical of this elevation.

From the trailhead at Ruby's Inn, follow the Rim Trail for about 0.4 mi. (0.6 km.), to a marked trail intersection. At this point, the Bryce Town Loop takes off through the forests, toward the south, beginning a nice climb up the oblong hill that is a prominent feature seen from the surrounding plateau flats. Continue up this hill to a low saddle within, which marks the beginning of a fast descent back down to the meadows in the flats in front of Ruby's Inn, which then return to the trailhead. Two rounds of this trail make for a great 10-km. (6.25-mi.) training workout, and is the course for the Ruby's Inn Winter Festival 5- and 10-km. ski and snowshoe races.

Tour 4: Inspiration–Bryce Points

Tour Length: 2.7 mi. (4.5 km.) round trip.

Difficulty: More difficult intermediate backcountry route. Although short, this trail follows a higher surface on the Paunsagunt Plateau, upon which there are several stretches of narrow trail with steep ascents and descents. The trail near the end at Bryce Point is particularly precipitous. Although this tour can be difficult going at times, the scenery is certainly worth the effort. The route is neither groomed nor marked for winter travel. Although a somewhat difficult ski, this route is highly recommended for snowshoers.

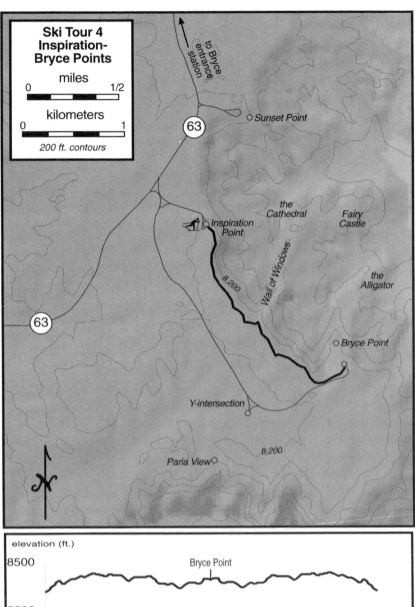

Elevation: 8,140–8,320 ft. (2,510–2,570 m.).

Snow Conditions: Typically snow covered between December and March. However, the entire rim can occasionally be entirely bare of snow during the depths of winter. Best months are February and March. Check with Ruby's Inn or the National Park Service for local conditions.

Geological and Other Scenic Features: A nice tour atop the White Limestone Member, which caps the Red Member of the Claron Formation. Some of the more spectacular views all along the trail include the "Cathedral," the "Wall of Windows," the "Alligator," and the "Fairy Castle."

Other Useful Maps: National Park Service Map "Bryce Canyon National Park," Trails Illustrated Map "Bryce Canyon National Park," and U.S. Geological Survey 7.5-minute Quadrangle "Bryce Point."

How to Get There (Paunsagunt Plateau Area Map)

This tour is accessed from the parking area for Inspiration Point, within Bryce Canyon National Park. To get to Bryce Canyon, take Highway 63 south from Highway 12. Drive 3 mi. south to the entrance station to the park (be prepared to pay the current entrance fee). Continue on Highway 63 (which eventually dead-ends within the park) about 2.5 mi. to a forked intersection. Take the left fork toward Inspiration, Bryce, and Paria View Points. Shortly after this intersection is a similar fork, where you will turn off into the Inspiration Point parking area.

If you do not want to do this as an out-and-back tour, you may choose to leave a second car at Bryce Point (but remember this means paying entrance fees for two vehicles). To do so, continue on the short road after the first turnoff about 1.4 mi. to the end at Bryce Point. The highway is generally plowed to Bryce Point, although the turnoff to Paria View point is not.

Ski Tour Description

Although there are several difficult stretches of trail with a few obstacles, this route offers some of the most scenic views in the park—many outside of the marked and commonly seen viewpoints. Because of the trail difficulties, this tour is really ideal for those on snowshoes, who will easily travel some of the steeper and woodsier sections.

From the Inspiration Point parking area, ski south along the canyon rim, entering the woods, and ascending a steep grade at first. It may seem as if skins would be necessary to make this ascent straight up, but it can easily be done with a few quick switchbacks. After climbing up to the high surface (about 200 ft., 30 m. of elevation gain) you are well above the surrounding plateau. Note that you are climbing atop a thick white sedimentary bed—the White Limestone Member of the Claron Formation. Once you reach this upper surface, continue to ski or snowshoe along the highest point, staying near the rim and traversing three small gullies that descend to the east. At the fourth gully, the road to Bryce Point can be seen. It is easier at this point to descend to the road grade and ski on or alongside the roadcut. The other alternative is to climb the steep hill just to the east of Bryce Point, and find a good track down. There are a few nice clear slopes for a few short tele turns if you do so. At either of these points continue slightly west to the rim at Bryce Point. Note that if you descend the trail to the actual viewpoint (about 1/8 mi. beyond the parking area and low fence), do so in ski boots, or on snowshoes, as the trail is very narrow, with steep slopes on either side.

Tour 5: Paria Loop

Tour Length: 3.1 mi. (5.2 km.) loop.

Difficulty: Beginner route. Although not groomed for freestyle skiing, this route is generally set with a nice set of tracks for easy classical skiing. The trail is clear and well marked with blue diamonds by the Park Service. The terrain is very gentle—all making for a nice leisurely ski through the woods.

Elevation: 7,920–8,120 ft. (2,440–2,500 m.).

Snow Conditions: Typically snow covered between December and March. February and March are best for snow conditions. These slightly higher elevation areas inside the park retain significantly more snow than those near Ruby's Inn. Check with the National Park Service for conditions.

Geological and Other Scenic Features: Gentle tours through the open Ponderosa pine forests of the Paunsagunt Plateau.

Other Useful Maps: National Park Service Map "Bryce Canyon National Park," Trails Illustrated Map "Bryce Canyon National Park," and U.S. Geological Survey 7.5-minute Quadrangle "Bryce Point."

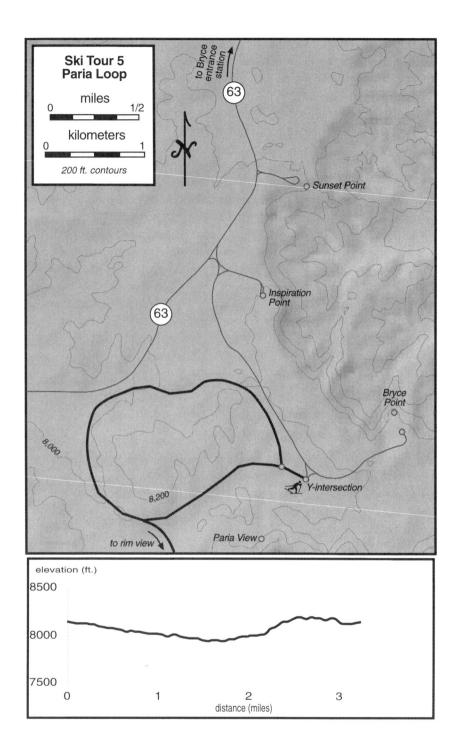

Near Paria View viewpoint

How to Get There (Paunsagunt Plateau Area Map)

This trail is accessible from the parking area at the Y-shaped intersection that diverges to Bryce Point and Paria View. See Tour 4—Inspiration–Bryce Points, for directions to Inspiration Point. After passing the turnoff to Inspiration Point, continue about 1 mi. (1.6 km.) to the second of the forked Y-intersections. Road plowing within the park varies from year to year with conditions, so the road to Bryce Point may or may not be plowed beyond this intersection. The short section of road to Paria View point is never plowed, except for a few hundred feet to allow for skier parking.

Ski Tour Description

This trail is a beautiful classical ski through some of the more beautiful Ponderosa forests of the upper plateau. The snow is generally in good condition because of being in the woods. The classical tracks are generally in good condition, being set by the Park Service. Furthermore, the terrain is just right for a quick 5-km. (3.1-mi.) classical training route.

If you are snowshoeing this route, do not walk on the nicely set ski tracks, as this makes classical skiing very difficult.

Although the short trip to Paria View point (straight ahead, following the snowed-over road surface) is worth the short detour, this is not on the marked Paria Loop winter trail. To take the Paria Loop trail, ski to the northwest (leaving the parking area from the right side of road). Follow the tracks that begin to descend a shallow gully within a wide meadow. At the end of the meadow, the trail splits into a two-way loop. It is best to ski to the left, and return via the other trail. The left trail continues down a broad drainage to a wide-open meadow near the canyon rim. This makes a good place to ski off trail slightly to the rim for a nice view (see map). A second slight detour, following the rim up to the high plateaus to the south, provides unique views back at the viewpoint areas (toward Bryce Point; see map). The trail continues through this meadow, at the edge of the forest, wrapping around the side of a broad hill. Once the Highway 63 area is reached, the trail continues around this hill, a few hundred feet from the road, climbing slightly through open meadows toward Inspiration Point. The retour then follows through the woods along the edge of the Bryce Point road, to the trail divergence mentioned above. Two rounds of this quick loop make for an excellent 10-km. (6.2-mi.) classical training course.

Tour 6: Sunset to Tropic

Tour Length: 2.5 mi. (4.2 km.) one way.

Difficulty: More difficult intermediate backcountry tour. A combination of factors makes this a challenging but rewarding tour. The first section of trail (down the canyon wall) must be descended in ski boots or on snowshoes, and can be very slippery in icy conditions. This section of the trail is generally icy due to high foot traffic. A backpack with ski pockets is an excellent way to transport skis to the bottom. This frees up hands for using ski poles as support. The rest of the tour follows a gully, exiting the main amphitheater to the town of Tropic. This route is not marked for winter travel, and therefore requires a bit of bushwhacking and route finding.

Elevation: 8,000–6,880 ft. (2,470–2,120 m.).

Snow Conditions: Although the canyon rim is typically snow covered between December and March, a significant part of the lower portions

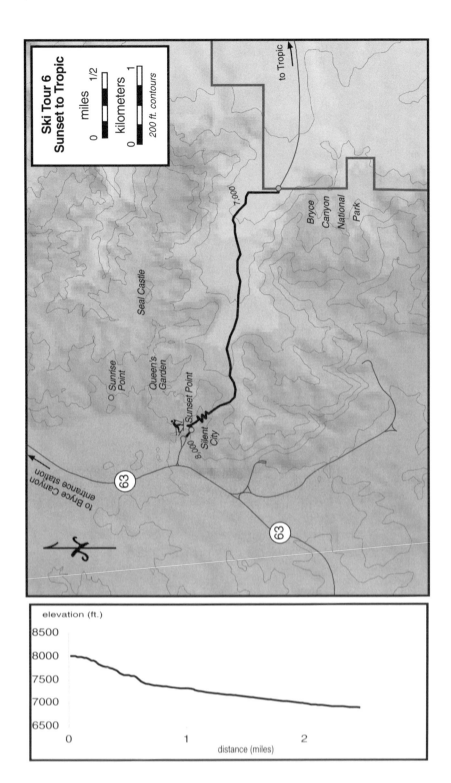

BRYCE CANYON; PAUNSAGUNT PLATEAU

of this tour may be barren. This may mean walking through a few short (or long) stretches. The snow on the first descent to the bottom is always thin and icy, so this portion should be walked carefully in ski boots with poles in hand.

Geological and Other Scenic Features: Up close and personal views of the fluvial deposits of the Claron Formation, as you descend through many of the hoodoos and narrow canyon walls.

Other Useful Maps: National Park Service Map "Bryce Canyon National Park," Trails Illustrated Map "Bryce Canyon National Park," and U.S. Geological Survey 7.5-minute Quadrangles "Bryce Canyon," "Bryce Point," "Cannonville," and "Tropic Canyon."

How to Get There (Paunsagunt Plateau Area Map)

This tour is accessed from the Sunrise Point parking area within Bryce Canyon National Park. Follow the directions in Ski Tour 4—Inspiration–Bryce Points, to the national-park entrance station. Continue 1.3 mi. (2.1 km.) to the turnout for Sunset Point.

Note that unless you want to ski back up to Sunset Point (not recommended), you will need to leave a second car outside the park, at the end of the access road in Tropic (the ending point of the ski tour). To get to this access point, continue on Highway 12 east from the intersection with Highway 63 until reaching the town of Tropic. In the center of the town, turn right on Bryce Road and continue several miles (as the road winds slightly) until this road reaches a dead-end and turn-around at a barbed-wire fence marking the park boundary. This fence will be your marker point for finding the car on the ski tour down. Use the ladder over the fence to avoid the treachery of barbs.

Ski Tour Description

This is probably the most interesting backcountry tour in the Bryce Canyon area. The trail traverses down the canyon walls through narrow slots, under bridges, to the bottom of the valley, with unique views back up at the plateau escarpment. Several slight walking or skiing detours make for unique and up-close viewpoints of the local red rocks of the Claron Formation. At times, the rim area can be overrun with tourists and buses, even in winter. But once you descend under the rim, you lose 99 percent of the crowd. This route also makes an excellent backcountry snowshoe tour.

From the Sunset Viewpoint parking area, walk or ski to the viewpoint (about 0.2 mi., 0.3 km.). At the viewpoint, follow the Navajo Loop trail (to the right) down the switchbacks under the rim and into the canyon. These switchbacks can be treacherous in icy conditions, when the snow has been packed by even a few walkers. It is best to carry a backpack with ski pouches, which will free up your hands to use your ski poles for stability. Boots with real soles are also advisable. Snowshoers should also carry poles to use in this slippery section. Near the bottom of the switchbacks, you will reach a giant leaning Ponderosa pine, thriving somehow within the narrow slot of the canyon. This is probably one of the most photographed points within Utah, and you have probably already seen many renditions of photographs in the gift shop at Ruby's Inn. Continue along the trail for about 300 ft. (100 m.), until you reach a good access point to the stream bottom. This stream can be followed down-canyon (more or less on either side) all the way to the park boundary fence, where the return car has been left. Otherwise it is a very long uphill climb back to Sunset Point. If you are not skiing within the stream bottom, a somewhat well-traveled trail, probably best for snowshoers, follows the right bank (looking down-canyon). However, the easiest ski route is right in the stream channel (which is dry).

Tour 7: Sunset Loop

Tour Length: 5.8 mi. (9.6 km.) loop.

Difficulty: A more difficult intermediate backcountry route. This tour is somewhat long, and it includes significant ascents and descents in the hilly country near the canyon rim. The trail is neither groomed nor marked, but it is well tracked, making route finding very easy.

Elevation: 7,760–8,160 ft. (2,290–2,520 m.).

Snow Conditions: Typically snow covered between December and March. The slightly higher elevation areas inside the park (about 8,100 ft.) retain significantly more snow than those near Ruby's Inn (about 7,700 ft.). Check with the National Park Service for local conditions.

Geological and Other Scenic Features: Some of the better viewpoints into Bryce Canyon, including Sunset Point, Sunrise Point, Fairyland Point, and others along the way. A climb to one of the highest peaks in the area, with nice views of the entire region.

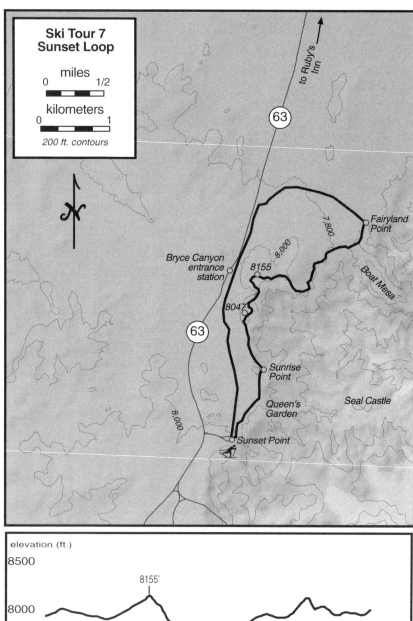
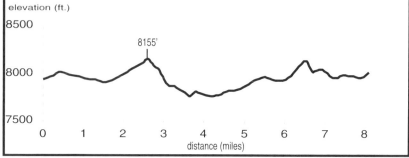

Fresh snow on the Paunsagunt

Other Useful Maps: National Park Service Map "Bryce Canyon National Park," Trails Illustrated Map "Bryce Canyon National Park," and U.S. Geological Survey 7.5-minute Quadrangles "Bryce Canyon" and "Bryce Point."

How to Get There (Paunsagunt Plateau Area Map)

This tour is accessed from the Sunset Point parking area within Bryce Canyon National Park. Follow the directions in Tour 6—Sunset to Tropic.

Ski Tour Description

This tour provides a great way to see some of the most widely photographed viewpoints within Bryce Canyon National Park, as well as others in the intervening country. This is a good trail for snowshoers, although the retour may be a bit long without the speed of skis.

From the Sunset Point parking area, ski north along the rim to Sunrise Point, the viewpoint visible up the hill from Sunset Point. From Sunrise Point, continue to follow the canyon rim, as close as possible without being too close. The trail first goes behind the sharp hill (elevation 8,047 ft. on USGS quadrangle), and then continues to climb along the rim to the high point of the area (elevation 8,155 ft.). This is a great point to take a break and see the surrounding area. The trail then descends to the north, losing almost 400 ft. (125 m.) in elevation, on some fairly steep slopes with a few possibilities for some quick turns —especially nice if the snow is right. Most of the year, however, the snow here is crusty due to wind and sun exposure. Once the trail flattens out, you will reach Fairyland Point, where the tour returns via the snowed-over roadway toward Highway 63. Once you reach the highway area, continue alongside the road (there are usually tracks to follow) until you reach the visitor center and campground. Continue to find the most skiable route through the campground and lodge areas back to Sunset Point. This area is usually covered with many anastomosing tracks, so it is best to simply find the most economical route in retour.

Tour 8: Paria View–Bryce Loop

Tour Length: 2.7 mi. (4.5 km.) loop.

Difficulty: Easier intermediate backcountry route. Although ungroomed and unmarked, this route is easy to follow. There are a few short but challenging climbs that make this an intermediate tour.

Elevation: 8,180–8,280 ft. (2,520–2,550 m.)

Snow Conditions: Generally snow covered between December and March, although snow conditions vary annually. Best months for snow are February and March. Check with the National Park Service for current conditions.

Geological and Other Scenic Features: Two of the usual views into Bryce Canyon and the Paria River drainage (Paria View and Bryce Point), as well as many spectacular up-close views of the fluvial sediments of the Claron Formation.

Other Useful Maps: National Park Service Map "Bryce Canyon National Park," Trails Illustrated Map "Bryce Canyon National Park," and U.S. Geological Survey 7.5-minute Quadrangle "Bryce Point."

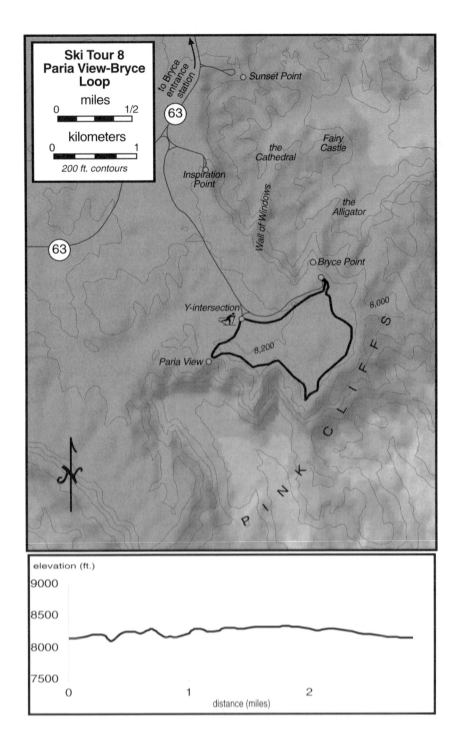

How to Get There (Paunsagunt Plateau Area Map)

This trail is accessible from the parking area at the Y-shaped intersection that diverges to Bryce Point and Paria View. See Tour 5—"Paria Loop" for detailed directions.

Ski Tour Description

This trail is a great way to escape some of the crowds during the busier winter times at Bryce. It is a little-known, quick, and easy tour that offers both spectacular views into the canyon and the solitude of the forested areas. It is also recommended for snowshoers.

From the trailhead, ski up the snowed-over road toward Paria View point. Just before the viewpoint is reached, there is a narrow and steep hill to the left. Climb this hill (switchbacking as necessary), and continue eastward along the edge of the cliff. There is one gully here to be crossed that will present something of a challenge, but this can be easily sidehilled. Once the highest hill is reached, follow down to the second gully and climb out to the broad flat area at the rim. Ski northward through the woods to the open area near the Bryce Point parking area, and continue to Bryce Point—one of the most spectacular views of Bryce Canyon. From here you can see many of the named features, such as the "Alligator," the "Wall of Windows," and the "Fairy Castle." Leave Bryce Point by following the broad drainage to the south of the road, through the open forests and meadows to the trailhead.

Tour 9: Casto Canyon

Tour Length: 4.2 mi. (7.0 km.) round trip.

Difficulty: Intermediate backcountry tour. Most of this trail is very gentle, but a few steep sections and tricky spots will be particularly challenging.

Elevation: 7,360–7,890 ft. (2,270–2,430 m.).

Snow Conditions: Because of its low elevation, snow conditions around Red Canyon can be spotty and highly variable. Following major storms, the snow stays around shortly afterwards, and is generally deep enough to ski. During good snow years, Red Canyon is extremely skiable. The best chances for good snow are in late February and March.

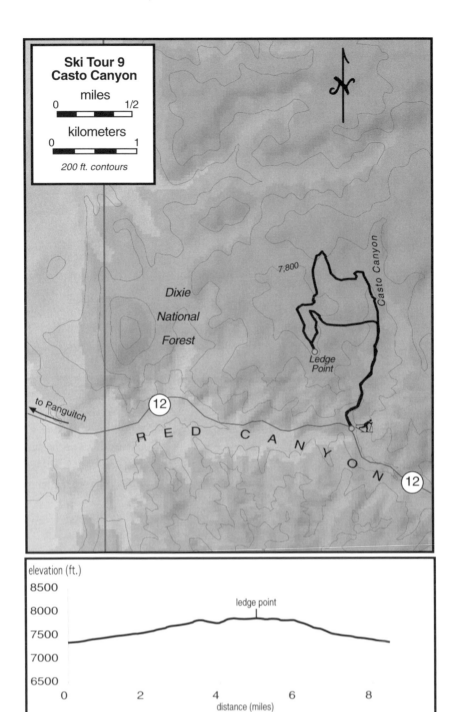

Geological and Other Scenic Features: Unique views of true canyons through the Claron Formation. Once the upper surfaces are reached, there are spectacular views of the surrounding areas: Brian Head, the Tushar Mountains, Sevier Plateau, and the Table Cliffs.

Other Useful Maps: Trails Illustrated Map "Paunsagunt Plateau" and U.S. Geological Survey 7.5-minute Quadrangles "Casto Canyon" and "Wilson Peak."

How to Get There (Paunsagunt Plateau Area Map)

This tour is located in the Red Canyon Recreation Area, along Scenic Highway 12 between Panguitch and Bryce Canyon. From Panguitch, drive east to the entrance of Red Canyon (when the rocks become a brilliant red color). About 0.5 mi. (0.8 km.) past the Red Canyon visitor station (closed in winter), is the trailhead. There is a picnic area, and restrooms within a short loop and parking area.

Ski Tour Description

The Red Canyon area, which is always passed on the way to Bryce Canyon, is often overlooked for the more popular recreation areas around Bryce. Only a few miles from the entrance of Bryce Canyon National Park, this entire area (with no entrance fee) offers a wide array of backcountry touring opportunities that follow summer hiking trails, only one of which is described in detail here, but many of which are very skiable. The Casto Canyon tour, while often poorly skiable because of spotty and thin snow conditions, makes for a great tour on a pair of lightweight, racing-style snowshoes, which tromp easily through the thin snow.

   From the Cassidy Trail trailhead and parking ski up the canyon, generally staying within the stream bottom. The trail passes from side to side of the stream, but is often exposed in bright sun, and barren of snow, making the stream bottom the best course to travel. After about 1.5 mi. (2.4 km.), there is a turnoff sign toward Ledge Point. Pass this sign and continue for another 0.5 mi. (.8 km.) to an easy access point up to the surrounding mesa, which follows the Rich Trail. Continue along this trail to the top of the plateau, from which there are spectacular views of the entire region. From this surface one can see the Markagunt Plateau (see Ski Touring Area 2), the Tushar Mountains (see Ski Touring Area 3), Mount Dutton, and the Sevier Plateau to the north. Continue to ski along the Rich Trail to a signpost marking a short trail to Ledge Point. From Ledge Point, return to the signpost, and travel on the Ledge Point trail down a narrow gully back to the main canyon. This should return to the Ledge Point turnoff 1.5 mi. (2.4 km.) up from the trailhead. From here you can ski back down the trail in return to the trailhead, although there is much possibility for further exploration.

Additional Resources:

Ruby's Inn
Accommodations, restaurants, rentals, repairs, grooming, snow conditions, etc.
Highway U-63
Bryce, UT 84764
1 (800) 468-8660
1 (435) 834-5341
http://www.rubysinn.com

Bryce Canyon National Park
National Park information, snowshoe rentals, local conditions
P. O. Box 170001
Bryce Canyon, UT 84717
(435) 834-5322
http://www.nps.gov/brca/

Dixie National Forest
Road conditions, weather, campgrounds, permits
USDA Forest Service
Cedar City District
(435) 865-3204
jwhicker@fs.fed.us
http://www.fs.fed.us/outernet/dixie_nf/welcome.htm

AREA 2

Cedar Breaks and Surroundings, Including Brian Head Ski Resort and Cedar Breaks National Monument

Cenozoic Plateau Building and Quaternary Volcanoes on the Markagunt Plateau

At elevation well above 10,000 ft. (3,050 m.), the upper rim of the Markagunt Plateau offers some of the finest, yet least widely popularized, cross-country skiing in the state. Because of its high elevation, the winter trails of the Markagunt Plateau offer a sometimes necessary alternative to the more popular touring areas around Bryce Canyon, where snow conditions can be occasionally spotty, even in midwinter. When the snow gods have not been good to Bryce, the Cedar Breaks area is less than 60 mi. away, and abundant snow is almost guaranteed between December and March. All of the Markagunt Plateau tours are within short driving distance from local population centers such as Cedar City and St. George, making for perfect day trips. For "outsiders," very convenient accommodations are available at nearby Brian Head Ski Resort, a great launching point for the Brian Head and Cedar Breaks area.

Although the landscape is similar to that of Bryce Canyon, the Markagunt Plateau is a lesser known, but perhaps more scenically attractive, area. The pinnacle of red rock skiing on the Markagunt Plateau is found at Cedar Breaks National Monument, where one can find splendid views into an immense natural amphitheater featuring mystical exposures of weathered rocks, which have been variously called "spires," "columns," "arches," "hoodoos," "goblins," "chessmen," or whatever else you may want to call the mysterious features exposed at the "breaks." The name "Cedar Breaks" was given to the natural amphitheater by early European settlers, who named it for the badland exposures, or "breaks," which are often vegetated with Utah juniper (*Juniperus osteosperma*). This arid-adapted tree is sometimes called "cedar," and is more abundant lower in the canyon of Ashdown Gorge. However, the local Native Americans had a more descriptive (and perhaps more clever) name for this vista, calling it the "Circle of Painted Cliffs."

Although the scenery is similar to that of Bryce Canyon, the Markagunt Plateau rim is higher in elevation, leaving most of the forests on the western rim near treeline. The forests are more open, and consist of stands of stunted Engelmann spruce (*Picea engelmanni*) and Subalpine fir (*Abies labiocarpa*), with dense thickets of quaking aspen (*Populus tremuloides*). The keen natural observer may find a few Bristlecone pine (*Pinus longaeva*, or "Methuselah" pine), one of the natural wonders of this unique environment. These trees often have a fascinatingly contorted and weathered appearance, like that of Bonsai trees, because they are one of the few species able to eke out a slow and meager existence in the harsh conditions of these high-elevation plateaus, especially at the rim of the Pink Cliffs. Most remarkable and photogenic specimens can be found at the plateau edge near Spectra Point (see Ski Tour 12) and on the "Gnarly Grove" tour (see Ski Tour 18). The oldest Bristlecones known in the Cedar Breaks area have been dated to at least 1,650 years old, and have therefore been alive since the times of the Mayan and Roman Empires. Although this age may seem impressive, especially for such small and stunted-looking trees, the Bristlecones of southern Utah are not nearly as old as some specimens in the White Mountains of California, the oldest of which have been dated to nearly 4,600 years before present—living trees as old as the Egyptian Pyramids! These are a species of truly remarkable survivors.

The winter trails of the Markagunt Plateau have something to offer for all types of winter tourers. First and foremost is the spectacular scenery, best enjoyed at the casual pace of ski touring or snowshoeing. The majority of the winter trails described in this section are designed to encompass at least one viewpoint of red rock exposures at the western plateau escarpment (Cedar Breaks National Monument and Brian Head Ski Resort areas). In addition to the relatively well-known Cedar Breaks/Brian Head area, this section describes several less frequented tours to some of the unique volcanic features of the lower Markagunt Plateau, such as Mammoth Cave, the Kolob Overlook, and some very recent lava fields near Navajo and Panguitch Lakes. Because the area sees relatively few tourists in winter, all of this scenery can be enjoyed

Leaves and bark of the Bristlecone pine (*Pinus longaeva*)

with as much solitude as one desires. Backcountry and telemark skiers will appreciate some of the great powder (450 inches average annual snowfall at the base of Brian Head Ski Resort), and the untracked terrain of the Brian Head, Navajo, and Lightning Point tours.

Geology of the Markagunt Plateau

The Markagunt Plateau is the "top step" in the "Grand Staircase" of sedimentary strata that characterizes the Grand Canyon–Zion–Bryce Canyon region of national parks. A great deal of this colorful staircase can be seen from the perspective of the ski tours along the Markagunt Plateau rim, especially well from the 11,307-ft. (3,446-m.) elevation at Brian Head Peak (see Ski Tour 16).

A trip through these giant geological steps can be envisioned as traveling up through the geological time scale (see geological time scale on page 3). This colorful ascent through time begins atop the rim of the Grand Canyon, where the Chocolate Cliffs are formed by outcrops of the Moenkopi Formation (Early Triassic). The staircase continues by stepping through the Vermillion Cliffs of the Moenave and Kayenta Formations (Late Triassic), the White Cliffs of the Navajo Sandstone (Triassic–Jurassic), the Grey Cliffs of the Straight Cliffs Formation (Cretaceous), and ends with the Pink Cliffs of the Claron Formation (Eocene) on the high Markagunt Plateau (for more details of the Claron Formation geology, see the description of the Paunsagunt Plateau in Ski Touring Area 1).

While the stratigraphic steps of the Grand Staircase generally trend west-by-southwest, the region is also intersected by a series of major faults that trend roughly north-by-northeast, thereby intersecting the cliff-forming steps at about right angles. One could take a geological trip similar to that described above, but in the opposite direction, through the steps of this fault system. This trip would begin from the west, with the first geological step up the Grand Wash Fault to the Shivwits Plateau and Pine Valley Mountains. One would then follow through successive steps up the Hurricane Fault to the Markagunt Plateau and Uinkaret Mountains (this section), up the Sevier (or Toroweap) Fault to the Kolob and Paunsagunt Plateaus (see Ski Touring Area 1), and finally up the East Kaibab Monocline (a steep bend in the rocks, and much like a fault) to the high Aquarius, Table Cliffs, and Boulder Mountain Plateaus (see Ski Touring Area 4).

Because the timing of the displacement on these faults (sometime after the Oligocene) postdates the deposition of the sedimentary strata (Eocene and earlier), the fault planes offset the stratigraphic steps of the Grand Staircase, thereby forming the "patchwork" geological map of southwest Utah. The curious intersection of these two orthogonal systems of cliffs—those formed by erosion of sedimentary strata, with those formed by the staircase of fault systems—has created the intricate tapestry of plateaus in this part of what can be called the greater Colorado Plateaus region. Each of these plateau surfaces has a unique orientation, which is determined chiefly by two factors, the sense of the fault that bounds the plateau edge and the dip of the strata that underlie the plateau surface.

In the case of the Markagunt Plateau, the west-bounding Hurricane Fault is upthrown to the east (the plateau side), thereby forming the escarpment at the western plateau margin, and producing the badland cliffs facing west at Cedar Breaks. The Claron Formation, the rock that underlies the plateau surface, dips eastward, producing the gently rising plateau surface, like a giant west-rising ramp toward Cedar Breaks. As the route of Highway 143 approaches Cedar Breaks from Panguitch, it approximates the surface formed by the top of the Claron limestones,

Claron formation exposures in the Hurricane fault at Cedar Breaks

which are relatively resistant to erosion and thereby "hold up" the plateau's ramping surface. This orientation contrasts with the plateau surface formed by the Claron Formation at Bryce Canyon, where the strata dip very gently to the west, and the fault bounds the exposures on the east.

Intimately associated with the displacement of the Hurricane Fault are copious volcanic features such as the lava flows and cinder cones that dot the plateau surface. Looking throughout the entire region, these recently erupted (Quaternary) volcanic rocks can be seen to follow a distinctive trend, roughly tracing the Hurricane Fault from northern Arizona to Parowan. Because this major active fault has fractured rocks deep into Earth's crust, the resulting zone of weakness has encouraged the ascent of magma from the depths of the mantle, through networks of fractures, to be extruded and cooled at the surface as basaltic lava flows and cinder cones. Several cinder cones can be seen from high viewpoints in the Cedar Breaks area and at Miller Knoll (see Ski Tour 19). Very fresh lava flows can be experienced in the Black Rock Desert (see Ski Tour 19), the Navajo Lake area (see Ski Tour 22), and around Mammoth Cave (see Ski Tour 21). Although this and many of the lava fields on the Markagunt Plateau look like they cooled yesterday, there is no clear historical record, or oral tradition, of Native Americans of any recent volcanic activity. This is surprising to many geologists, who recognize the evidence of very little lichen growth (often used to accurately date very young geological surfaces of exposure).

These sorts of basaltic volcanic features are characteristic of the areas fringing the Basin and Range Province, a region known by its active crustal extension. At the margins of the Basin and Range, heat flow from the mantle is greatly increased, resulting in the abundant volcanism. These very recent outpourings of basaltic lava (which include more extensive flows of the Snake River Plains of Idaho and the High Lava Plains of Oregon) trace the outline of one of Earth's many "rings of fire," and delineate the margins of this tectonically active region.

Area 2 Ski Tours

Map No.	Ski Tour	Length in mi. (km.)*	Difficulty and Notes*
Cedar Breaks National Monument Area			
10	Alpine Pond	3.4 mi. (5.5 km.) RT	B (BC, S)
11	Chessmen Ridge Overlook	4.5 mi. (7.2 km.) RT	B (BC, S)
12	Spectra Point	10.3 mi. (16.6 km.) RT	I–A (BC, S)
Brian Head Ski Resort Area			
13	North Rim	1.7 mi. (2.7 km.) LP	B
14	Lightning Point	1.9 mi. (3.0 km.) RT	I (T)
15	Navajo Point	3.4 mi. (5.4 km.) RT	I–A (T)
Brian Head Area Backcountry Tours			
16	Brian Head Peak	5.6 mi. (9.0 km.) RT	A (BC; T)
17	Pioneer Cabins	4.2 mi. (6.8 km.) RT	B–I
18	The "Gnarly Grove"	8.8 mi. (14.0 km.) RT	A (BC)
Other Areas			
19	Miller Knoll	4.3 mi. (6.8 km.) RT	B–I (BC)
20	Kolob Plateau Overlook	7.1 mi. (11.4 km.) RT	I (BC)
21	Mammoth Cave	5.0 mi. (8.0 km.) RT	B
22	Markagunt Lava Fields	2.6 mi. (4.2 km.) RT	B (S)

*RT = Round trip; LP = Loop; B = Beginner; I = Intermediate; A = Advanced; BC = Backcountry route, unmarked trail; S = Also recommended for snowshoes; T = Telemark possibilities.

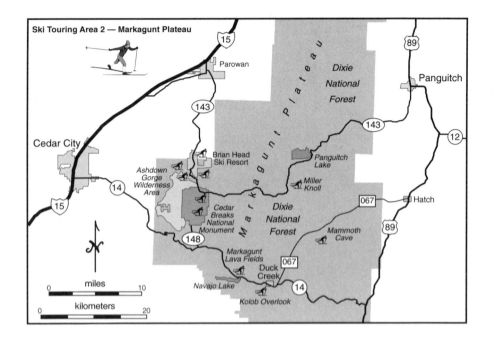

Tour 10: Alpine Pond

Tour Length: 3.4 mi. (5.5 km.) round trip.

Difficulty: Moderately difficult backcountry beginner route. Although the terrain is rather gentle, some narrow sections of trail with a few steep climbs and tight fits between obstacles will present significant challenges to the skills of beginning skiers. However, this trail is highly recommended for snowshoers of all levels, who will easily manage these challenging sections.

Elevation: 10,500–10,600 ft. (3,210–3,270 m.).

Snow Conditions: Nearly always covered with several feet of snow between December and March (occasionally skiable from early October to June). Note that strong winds during extended periods without snowfall can cause bare spots as well as crusty and icy snow, especially near the plateau edge.

Geological and Other Scenic Features: Magnificent exposures of lake and river deposits (limestone, shale, and sandstone) of the Eocene Claron Formation. Views of Late Quaternary cinder cones and lava-covered plateau surface.

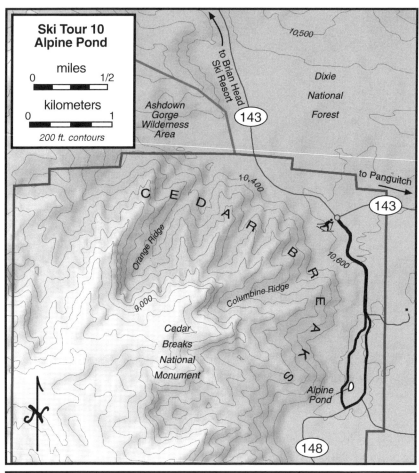
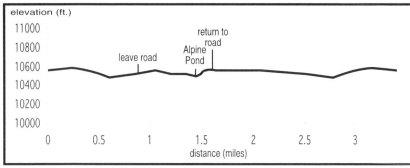

Other Useful Maps: National Park Service Map "Cedar Breaks National Monument," U.S. Geological Survey 7.5-minute Quadrangle "Brian Head."

How to Get There (Markagunt Plateau Area Map)

The parking area and trailhead for all ski tours in the Cedar Breaks area lies at the north entrance to the monument, where Utah State Highway 143 (open in winter) intersects Highway 148 (closed). If approaching from U.S. Highway 89 via Panguitch, drive west on State Highway 143, past Panguitch Lake, toward Brian Head Ski Resort. The intersection with Highway 148 is marked by a stop sign and right turn toward Brian Head and Parowan. To the left, Highway 148 passes through Cedar Breaks National Monument, but is closed in winter and is plowed a few hundred feet past the intersection to provide parking for skiers, snowshoers, and snowmobilers. Ski tours 10–12 in the monument begin by following the snowed-over highway grade.

To access the Cedar Breaks area from the west, exit Interstate 15 at Parowan (exit 78 from the north, exit 75 from the south) on State Highway 143. Follow this through Parowan, past Brian Head Ski Resort, to the intersection with Highway 148. Note that the winter trails through the monument are not accessible in winter via State Highways 148 and 14 from the south, as Highway 148 is not plowed.

Ski Tour Description

The Alpine Pond tour follows the Markagunt Plateau escarpment, through open meadows and groves of Engelmann spruce, Subalpine fir, and quaking aspen to a small, iced-over pond perched precariously on a shelf of the plateau escarpment. Although the summer hiking trail is marked, the ski and snowshoe touring route does not always follow directly along these trail markers, and the ski track typically varies slightly from year to year. If you are setting your own tracks after fresh snowfall, it is fairly easy to find one of the many easily skied routes through the forested backcountry to the pond, by simply keeping in the relatively open forest country between the plateau edge and the highway.

The first 0.25 mi. (0.4 km.) of trail follows the snowed-over highway grade (you can't miss the highway signs!), which is generally well packed with numerous snowmobile tracks. After the first gentle climb, the trail exits the forest into a fairly continuous, moderately steep descent with several unobstructed viewpoints of the exposures of Cedar Breaks to the right. At about 0.75 mi. (1.2 km.), the winter trail leaves the highway and follows through a broad, open meadow, descending slightly to the right. The summer marker for the hiking trail turnoff is another 0.1 mi. (0.2 km.) up the road, in case you miss this drainage. If you've gone this far, it is best to return to the meadow route. Follow to the end of the meadow, down a small drainage into the forests dominated by spruce and fir. At about 0.5 mi. (0.8 km.) after leaving the road, the trail ends up at a small opening in the trees—Alpine Pond, a great spot for a lunch stop. The pond was likely formed by dissolution of the uppermost limestone layer of the Claron Formation, as water has penetrated along a small fault that runs behind the pond. This fault has left the Alpine Pond surface as a small shelf at the plateau edge.

After crossing the pond surface, the trail climbs steeply southward and may be somewhat difficult to follow. Because the slopes are steep and heavily forested, this short section of trail presents the greatest challenge on this tour, as it winds through narrowly spaced trees, around rocks, and up a steep slope. Herringboning is an essential skill for these narrow climbs. Sidehill as necessary to the west, up about 60 ft. (20 m.), to the surface on which the highway sits. Once the highway is reached, the trail follows the road grade northward, around a low hill in return to the trailhead.

Tour 11: Chessmen Ridge Overlook

Tour Length: 4.5 mi. (7.2 km.) round trip.

Difficulty: Easiest beginner route. This tour offers gently rolling terrain and several viewpoints, and is very easy to follow by the well-traveled snowmobile and ski tracks along the snowed-over highway grade. The Alpine Pond tour, which follows roughly the same route, is more recommended for snowshoers of all levels, as it follows a more scenic route.

Elevation: 10,500–10,600 ft. (3,210–3,270 m.).

Snow Conditions: Nearly always covered with several feet of snow between December and March (occasionally skiable from early October to June). Note that strong winds during extended periods without snowfall can cause crusty and icy snow, especially near the plateau edge and on the downhill section, as noted below.

Geological and Other Scenic Features: Magnificent exposures of lake and river deposits (limestone, shale, and sandstone) of Eocene Claron

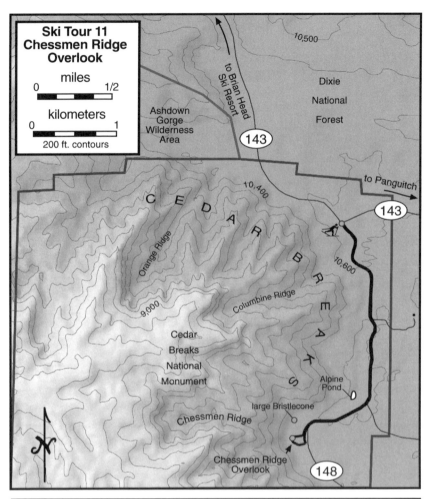

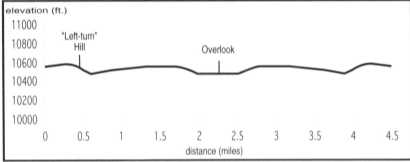

CEDAR BREAKS; MARKAGUNT PLATEAU

Formation. Views of Late Quaternary cinder cones and lava flows on plateau surface.

Other Useful Maps: National Park Service Map "Cedar Breaks National Monument," U.S. Geological Survey 7.5-minute Quadrangle "Brian Head."

How to Get There (Markagunt Plateau Area Map)

See directions for Ski Tour 10—Alpine Pond. Use the Cedar Breaks winter trailhead and parking area at the intersection of Highways 143 and 148.

Ski Tour Description

This route is designed as a beginner skier's alternative to the Alpine Pond tour, offering several picturesque viewpoints of Cedar Breaks, but circumventing the few difficult stretches of backcountry trail in the Alpine Pond tour. The entire route follows the grade of Highway 148, which is generally well-packed by snowmobile and ski travel. Although this well-traveled route makes for ease of skiing over "groomed" surfaces, crusty and wind-blown snow on anastomosing ski and snowmobile tracks can make turning difficult in some places.

   From the parking area, follow the tracks and highway grade southward, through the first stand of Engelmann spruce. After exiting the first stretch of forest, at the top of a gentle climb, the trail begins to descend a fairly long, continuous hill. This hill may offer a bit of speed for the brave beginner, but perhaps a bit too much speed for those less adventurous. To add to this challenge, the route takes a sharp left turn that can be difficult to manage, especially in the icy, uneven snow conditions that often exist through this section because of its proximity to the windy plateau edge. In particularly icy conditions, and for those uncomfortable with extended periods of uncontrolled velocity, this steep section can be easily averted by sidehilling to the east (into a very large, open meadow, where the snow is typically better) and simply returning to the highway grade farther along.

   After warding off the potential challenges of "Left-turn Hill," the trail follows the highway, rather uneventfully, through peaceful meadows and groves and over rolling terrain, to a ridge that extends into the Cedar Breaks amphitheater—Chessmen Ridge Overlook. This viewpoint offers some of the best vistas in the monument, with views of Chessmen, Columbine, and Orange Ridges, all aligned like battleships at dock. Although the described touring route returns to the trailhead via the same route, the inquisitive may find that, with a bit of extra time, a few short backcountry trips through the narrow forest belt to the plateau edge will prove rewarding with unique viewpoints. For example, at the cliff edge, just north of the Chessmen Ridge Overlook, is a fine specimen of an ancient Bristlecone pine (see map).

Tour 12: Spectra Point

Tour Length: 10.3 mi. (16.6 km.) round trip.

Difficulty: Long, moderately difficult backcountry route. Although the terrain is relatively gentle, this route is long, and should be attempted only with a full day of skiing, and with good weather and snow conditions. Most of the route follows snowmobile-groomed trails and highway markers through the monument. However, the last 0.7 mi. (1.1 km.) involves difficult backcountry route finding, negotiation of a few short, steep slopes, and potentially slippery slopes near the cliff edges. The advanced skiers' detour, or additional snowshoe route to Wasatch Ramparts, is recommended only for skiers with excellent stability and stamina.

Elevation: 10,200–10,600 ft. (3,110–3,230 m.).

Snow Conditions: Nearly always covered with several feet of snow between December and March (occasionally skiable from early October to June). Note that strong winds during extended periods without snowfall can cause crusty and icy snow. Snow conditions near the plateau edge, especially in the last 0.7 mi. (1.1 km.) between Point Supreme and Spectra Point, can be dangerous due to icy conditions near steep dropoffs. If such conditions exist, find alternate routes through the forest, a safe distance away from "the breaks."

Geological and Other Scenic Features: Full views of the entirety of Cedar Breaks, the Eocene Claron Formation. Also note a few small-scale faults within the sedimentary beds, especially visible from Spectra Point. These faults are parallel to, and part of, the massive Hurricane Fault system, which bounds the plateau's western edge.

Other Useful Maps: National Park Service Map "Cedar Breaks National Monument" and U.S. Geological Survey 7.5-minute Quadrangles "Brian Head" and "Navajo Lake."

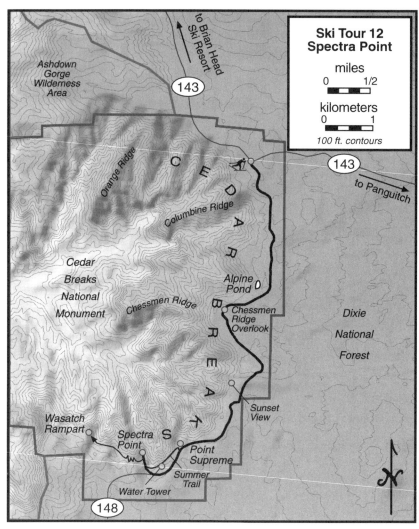

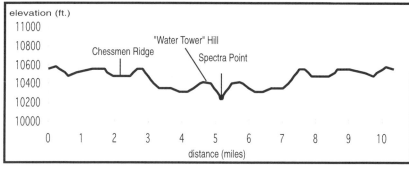

How to Get There (Markagunt Plateau Area Map)

See directions for Ski Tour 10—Alpine Pond. Use the Cedar Breaks winter trailhead and parking area at the intersection of Highways 143 and 148. Although one may be tempted by the somewhat shorter distance to access Spectra Point via the turnoff from Highway 14, this route is a much steeper climb, and does not offer the intervening scenery of the plateau route described here.

Ski Tour Description

This route is designed as an extended tour beyond the Chessmen Ridge Overlook, providing access to nearly all of Cedar Breaks National Monument's scenic viewpoints. Much of the tour follows the summer driving route along Highway 148, which is generally well packed by snowmobile and ski travel. The final 0.75 mi. (1.2 km.) is a backcountry route, approximating the summer hiking trail to Spectra Point, easily the most dramatic viewpoint at Cedar Breaks.

Follow the description of Tour 11 to Chessmen Ridge Overlook, and continue south along the highway grade. Although it provides less of a backcountry experience, following the highway grade is the easiest route through this section, as it is generally groomed by snowmobile trails, and thereby avoids trailbreaking through the longer stretches. About 0.75 mi. (1.2 km.) past Chessmen Ridge, the highway climbs and descends a sizable hill, the downhill portion of which offers the opportunity for a few quick turns, especially if one leaves the highway for the meadows below. After this hill, the route continues to follow the road grade, passing the turnoff to the summer campground. The tour then leaves the road grade at Point Supreme, the site of the monument's summer visitor center (closed in winter).

Although the summer trail to Spectra Point begins at the visitor-center parking lot, the first 0.25 mi. of the summer trail approaches too closely to the badlands escarpment to be skied safely. It is much more advisable to ski through a meadow, around the backside of a small hill ("water tower hill"). Begin this detour at the southern edge of the parking lot by skiing through the meadow, keeping a stand of trees between the skier and the cliff (see map). After passing the water tower (at the high point on the hill), work your way back near the plateau escarpment, swinging wide, down into a small drainage (which, incidentally, follows a fault plane). Follow this to a salient peninsula (Spectra Point) that extends a few hundred meters northward into "the breaks." On this ledge are several picturesque examples of ancient and very gnarled

Bristlecone pine, while many more can be found along the trail to Wasatch Rampart. Some of these make excellent photographic specimens.

The trail to Wasatch Rampart descends steeply through relatively dense forests, so it is left here as an "advanced skiers' backcountry detour." This detour is also ideal for snowshoers, as it requires greater maneuverability on some of the steeper slopes.

Tour 13: North Rim

Tour Length: 1.7 mi. (2.7 km.) loop.

Difficulty: Easy beginner loop route. Although not always well groomed or tracked in, this route is short and has few climbs—making it an ideal scenic route for new and beginner skiers.

Elevation: 10,400–10,540 ft. (3,170–3,210 m.).

Snow Conditions: Nearly always covered with several feet of snow between December and March (occasionally skiable from early October to June). Snow conditions at the viewpoint can be dangerous due to icy snow and steep dropoffs.

Geological and Other Scenic Features: Unique viewpoint of the Eocene Claron Formation of Cedar Breaks National Monument. A few ancient and contorted Bristlecone pine trees at plateau edge.

Other Useful Maps: Dixie National Forest "Travel Map" and U.S. Geological Survey 7.5-minute Quadrangle "Brian Head."

How to Get There (Markagunt Plateau Area Map)

The parking area and trailhead for the North Rim tour is approximately 1 mi. (1.6 km.) northwest of the intersection of Utah State Highways 143 and 148. Note that this is not the "North View Overlook" turnout and parking area within the national monument, but rather the unmarked trailhead area for the Rattlesnake Rim summer hiking trail, just outside the monument. If you are approaching from U.S. Highway 89 through Panguitch, drive west on State Highway 143, past Panguitch Lake, toward Brian Head Ski Resort. One mile (1.6 km.) past the Cedar Breaks winter parking area (at the intersection with Highway

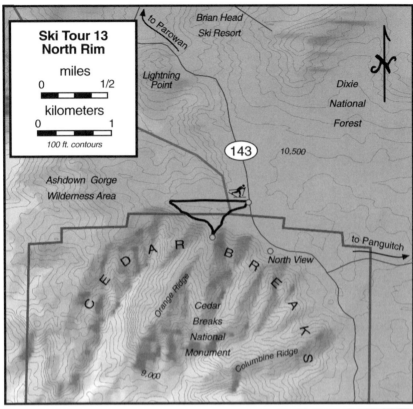

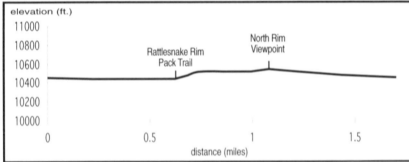

148), is the North Rim trailhead parking area, which is generally plowed by Brian Head Ski Resort, except in extreme conditions.

If approaching from the west, exit Interstate 15 at Parowan (exit 78 from the north, exit 75 from the south) on State Highway 143 toward Brian Head Ski Resort. Three mi. (4.8 km.) past Brian Head town center, and shortly after the turnoff sign to Brian Head Peak, is the North Rim trailhead parking area.

Ski Tour Description

This route begins with a pleasant ski through an open but isolated meadow, traveling due west along the Rattlesnake Rim summer trail to the plateau escarpment (the summer trail continues down into the canyon). Once this point is reached, follow the plateau edge southeast, to a small hill atop the cliff, which offers a splendid view into Cedar Breaks monument between Orange and Columbine Ridges. Keep an eye out for some of the Bristlecone pine trees, which are curiously always found growing in the harsh conditions within a few meters of the windy precipice, anywhere there are exposures of the Pink Cliffs of Claron Formation. From this hill, simply follow the plateau edge eastward toward the highway. One can follow this edge all the way to the "North View" drive-up summer overlook and return alongside the highway. However, at any point, a shortcut northward through the meadow will return you to the trailhead.

Tour 14: Lightning Point

Tour Length: 1.9 mi. (3.0 km.) round trip.

Difficulty: Short intermediate tour, with excellent opportunities for leisurely tele turns through the forested slopes of Lightning Point. Skiers should be comfortable with turning on relatively steep downhill sections.

Elevation: 10,000–10,400 ft. (3,050–3,170 m.).

Snow Conditions: Nearly always covered with several feet of snow between December and March (occasionally skiable from early October to June).

Geological and Other Scenic Features: 360-degree viewpoints of Cedar Breaks, Ashdown Gorge, and Brian Head Peak.

Other Useful Maps: Dixie National Forest "Travel Map" and U.S. Geological Survey 7.5-minute Quadrangle "Brian Head."

How to Get There (Markagunt Plateau Area Map)

The parking area and trailhead for the Lightning Point and Navajo Point touring area is 0.9 mi. (1.4 km.) south of Brian Head town center on Highway 143. This point is marked by a distinctively sharp turn

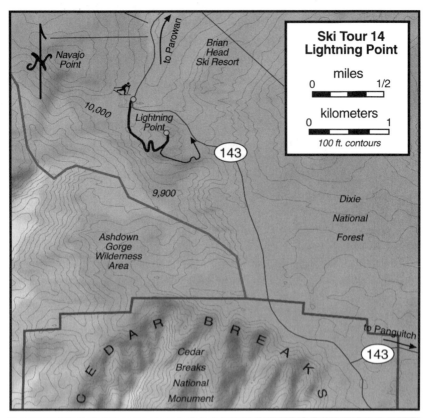

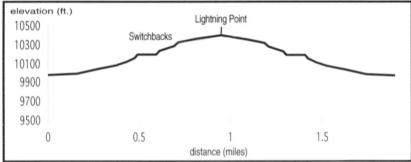

in the highway. If approaching from the west, exit Interstate 15 at Parowan (exit 78 from the north, exit 75 from the south) on State Highway 143 toward Brian Head Ski Resort. Just under a mile past the Brian Head Hotel is the trailhead parking area, plowed by the ski resort except in extreme conditions.

If you are approaching from U.S. Highway 89 through Panguitch, drive west on State Highway 143, past Panguitch Lake, toward Brian

Head Ski Resort. Three miles past the Cedar Breaks winter parking (at the intersection with Highway 148), is the Lightning Point and Navajo Point trailhead parking area.

Ski Tour Description

Although this tour is relatively short, the route provides access to some excellent (although somewhat short) tele skiing runs within the forested slopes. Despite its easy accessibility, the area is often free of tracks. While backcountry and telemark skiers will appreciate this as a playground, those looking for yet another scenic tour will enjoy some of the grand views of nearby Cedar Breaks, Ashdown Gorge, to as far as the Tushar Mountains and the Great Basin. Others may simply enjoy it as a short but vigorous climb.

From the trailhead area ski through the large meadow due south, until reaching a road that climbs through the forest and up the slope (near the edge of the rim that drops off into Cedar Breaks). This is a popular summer camping area, so do not be confused by several abruptly ending "turnoffs" into camping spots. After leaving the meadow, the trail climbs steeply, and begins a series of switchbacks up to the peak. Near the ridge top, a side trail takes off to the right. This route returns down the other side of Lightning Point, and is left as an alternate return to the highway (see map; shuttle vehicle necessary). Once on top of the peak, some of the best ski runs can be found in the forested area north of the switchbacks, all of which end up in the meadow near the trailhead and parking.

Tour 15: Navajo Point

Tour Length: 3.4 mi. (5.4 km.) round trip.

Difficulty: Relatively short intermediate tour, with excellent opportunities for tele turns through the trees, also providing access to some of the downhill terrain of Brian Head Ski Resort. The last steep climb (above the ski lift) is something of a challenge, and may require skins.

Elevation: 10,000–10,580 ft. (3,050–3,220 m.).

Snow Conditions: Nearly always covered with several feet of snow between December and March (occasionally skiable from early October to June).

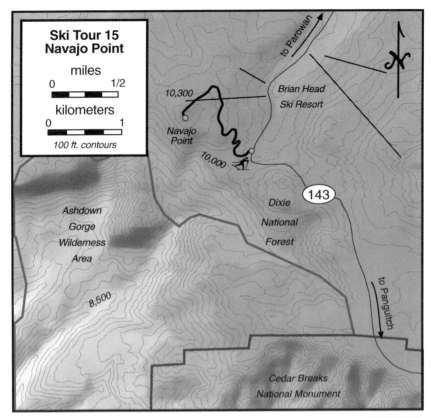

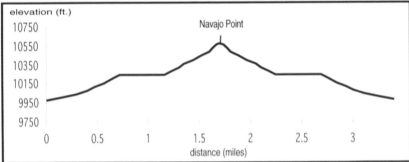

Geological and Other Scenic Features: 360-degree viewpoints of Cedar Breaks, Ashdown Gorge, and Brian Head Peak.

Other Useful Maps: Dixie National Forest "Travel Map" and U.S. Geological Survey 7.5-minute Quadrangle "Brian Head."

How to Get There (Markagunt Plateau Area Map)

See directions for Tour 14—Lightning Point. Use the Lightning Point/Navajo Point winter trailhead and parking area at the sharp bend in the highway.

Ski Tour Description

Navajo Point provides a great launching point for some of the backcountry and telemark skiing country of Brian Head Ski Resort. Besides some of the great downhill, the peak provides great views of the surrounding areas and a challenging climb.

From the parking area ski west through the meadow to a forest road that begins to climb the shoulder of Navajo Point. This road climbs steadily through thick forests of Engelmann spruce and Subalpine fir with a few areas of recent clear-cut. When the trail reaches the shoulder, the forest opens up to the ski runs of Brian Head Resort. The trail through this section follows cat tracks under the Navajo lift. Continue along the cat tracks to nearly the top of the lift, and begin climbing the northern slopes of the peak. This portion of trail is steep and heavily forested, and will require careful switchbacking and trailbreaking skills. In deep snow conditions, the last section of trail will be much easier with skins. From this point (or if you elect to stop at the top of the lift), there is a great deal of backcountry and downhill terrain. Find the most pleasurable way down. If you follow the runs to the bottom of the lifts, you will either end up hoofing it back to the trailhead (a long walk), or will benefit from having left a shuttle vehicle at the resort.

Tour 16: Brian Head Peak

Tour Length: 5.6 mi. (9.0 km.) round trip (plus additional backcountry mileage).

Difficulty: More difficult backcountry route. Icy snow and windy conditions can make this route much more difficult than it may seem. Advanced backcountry and telemark skiers will find several options for downhill routes from this point. Skins may be necessary in some conditions for the steeper sections of trail.

Elevation: 10,400–11,300 ft. (3,170–3,440 m.).

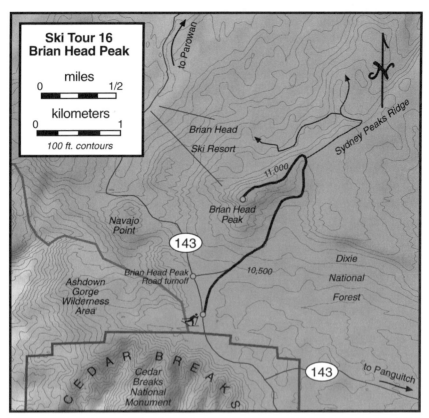
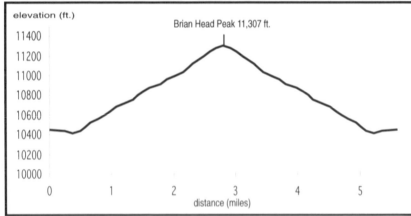

Snow Conditions: Nearly always covered with several feet of snow between December and March (occasionally skiable from early October to June). In places, snow can be windblown and icy. Avalanche conditions may exist, especially on the section of trail below the steep southern slopes of Brian Head Peak and in the backcountry areas of Brian Head resort. Skiers should be prepared with avalanche techniques and equipment, and should check with the Ski Patrol at Brian Head for up-to-date avalanche information.

Geological and Other Scenic Features: Easily the most expansive viewpoint of the entire region, with views of seemingly endless terrain. On a clear day, one can see hundreds of miles into the Basin and Range topography, as far as Wheeler Peak, in Great Basin National Park of Nevada, and all the way to the Kaibab Plateau in northern Arizona.

Other Useful Maps: Dixie National Forest "Travel Map" and U.S. Geological Survey 7.5-minute Quadrangle "Brian Head."

How to Get There (Markagunt Plateau Area Map)

See directions for Ski Tour 13—North Rim. Because there is no plowed parking at the Brian Head road turnoff, use the North Rim winter trailhead and parking area. Ski 0.25 mi. (0.4 km.) through the meadow, roughly along the highway to the beginning of the Brian Head Peak road.

Ski Tour Description

Brian Head Peak is the highest point on the Markagunt Plateau (11,307 ft./3,446 m.), and on a clear day offers expansive views of the surrounding area. Because of the lack of summer traffic and congestion, the winter air in southwest Utah is extremely clean, adding to this amazing visibility. Spring is often the best season for this tour, as the peak is most often shrouded in clouds during the winter months.

Starting from the North Rim trailhead, ski through the large open meadow, following along some of the snowmobile tracks in a northeasterly direction. Continue along contours until reaching an easy access point on the snowed-over Brian Head Peak road. The road is often skied-in and provides a good skiing surface, but can be difficult to follow precisely in deep snow conditions. Continue in a generally northeastward direction, climbing constantly to a ravine that climbs toward Sydney Peaks Ridge, which then ramps westward to the summit. After reaching the saddle, climb the ramping plateau surface to the peak shelter (one of the many recreational structures built by the Civilian Conservation Corps in the 1930s).

The peak can be extremely windy, and white-outs are frequent in the depths of winter. If it is clear, to the west one can see the edge of the Colorado Plateau Region and the transition to the Basin and Range Province (this boundary is the Hurricane Fault). Wheeler Peak (13,063 ft./3,982 m.), a large pyramidal mountain on the far skyline (in Nevada), stands out like a sore thumb among the other low ranges. To the north, the glaciated bowls of Mount Baldy, Mount Belknap, and Delano Peak stand out above the rest of the Tushar Range. To the south, one can look down the Grand Staircase and see as far as the Kaibab Plateau on the North Rim of the Grand Canyon.

From this point, the easiest retour to the trailhead is via the same route. However, Brian Head Peak is an excellent launching point for more adventurous backcountry touring, and provides access to some great telemark terrain (see map). To access the backcountry of upper Brian Head Resort (Giant Steps and Roulette lifts), continue to ski northeast along the Sydney Peaks Ridge line to a narrow break in the cliffs, about 0.5 mi. (0.8 km.) from the sharp turn at the saddle. From here, one can descend into the Pioneer Cabins area (see Ski Tour and Map 17), or traverse the ridge to the backcountry and tree runs above the lifts. Note that either of these options requires knowledge of, and equipment for, avalanche safety. Of course, if you decide to ski one of these backcountry routes, plan on leaving a shuttle vehicle at the resort for the return to the trailhead parking.

Tour 17: Pioneer Cabins

Tour Length: 4.2 mi. (6.8 km.) round trip (plus additional backcountry mileage).

Difficulty: Beginner route to cabins. More difficult intermediate mileage beyond cabins. The beginning of this tour follows the only well-groomed trail in the Brian Head area. Additional backcountry mileage on this tour involves some significant climbs, as well as one steep downhill section, and will require various route-finding and trail-breaking skills, depending on conditions. Several advanced backcountry routes are marked for those skiers seeking some of the untracked terrain, with powdery downhill sections.

Elevation: 9,480–9,840 ft. (2,890–3,000 m.).

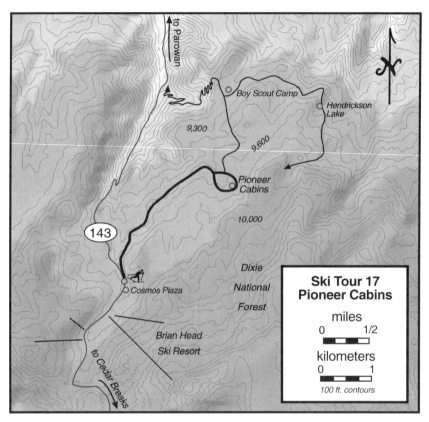

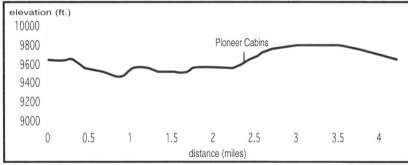

Snow Conditions: Generally snow covered between December and March (occasionally from October to late May). Snow on the backcountry route from the Boy Scout Camp to Highway 143 may be patchy in later months.

Geological and Other Scenic Features: Views down into Parowan Canyon. Historic cabins built by early settlers of the area.

Pioneer cabins on the Markagunt Plateau

Other Useful Maps: Dixie National Forest "Travel Map" and U.S. Geological Survey 7.5-minute Quadrangle "Brian Head."

How to Get There (Markagunt Plateau Area Map)

The parking area and trailhead for the Pioneer Cabins tour is 0.5 mi. (0.8 km.) south of the Brian Head Hotel on Highway 143, just north of the Cosmos Plaza. If approaching from the west, exit Interstate 15 at Parowan (exit 78 from the north, exit 75 from the south) to State Highway 143 toward Brian Head Ski Resort. Just before the Cosmos Plaza, there is a plowed parking area from which snowmobiles access several cabins farther up the road.

If approaching from U.S. Highway 89 through Panguitch, drive west on State Highway 143, past Brian Head Ski Resort. Just after the Cosmos Plaza is the parking and trailhead.

Ski Tour Description

This groomed track provides access to some historic cabins built by some of the first settlers in the Brian Head area. Beyond the groomed route, advanced backcountry skiers will find this route a great launching point for some downhill terrain (generally through forested areas with a few open meadows), with two possibilities for add-on backcountry skiing shown on the map.

The groomed part of the tour begins by traveling up the snowed-over road and continues in the same direction through the forest, climbing along ledges on the side of the slope. After about 3.5 mi. (5.8 km.), the trail drops quickly down into a small meadow area. The trail does a loop around this meadow, passing by the Pioneer Cabins. The groomed trail then loops back on itself and returns via the same route.

Two additional backcountry add-on routes extend from the Pioneer Cabins area (see map). For the Boy Scout Camp/Parowan Canyon route, ski to the north end of the Pioneer Cabins meadow, to a forest road that descends to the north (toward the Scout camp). After reaching the camp, follow a road beginning at the north end of the camp, which descends through several long switchbacks to Parowan Canyon. This route definitely requires a shuttle, as it is a long, steep walk back up to Brian Head.

The second backcountry route past Hendrickson lake is much longer, and begins again by passing through the Boy Scout Camp. Instead of descending into Parowan canyon, head east along a pack trail to Hendrickson Lake. From Hendrickson Lake, climb the series of ridges to the shelf that sits above the Pioneer Cabins meadow, and return via the subdivisions as described above.

Tour 18: The Gnarly Grove

Tour Length: 8.8 mi. (14.0 km.) round trip.

Difficulty: Long, most difficult backcountry route with substantial elevation gain and loss. Although much of the route may often be groomed by snowmobiles, the last 0.5 mi. (0.8 km.) requires off-track, backcountry skiing skills and negotiation of short, steep climbs within somewhat dense forests. This portion of the trail falls within the Ashdown Gorge Wilderness Area, and it is therefore unmarked and often untracked (as snowmobiles are not allowed), requiring trail-breaking and the use of skins in some conditions.

Elevation: 9,560–10,280 ft. (2,910–3,130 m.).

Snow Conditions: Generally snow covered between December and March (occasionally from October to late May).

Geological and Other Scenic Features: Spectacular grove of

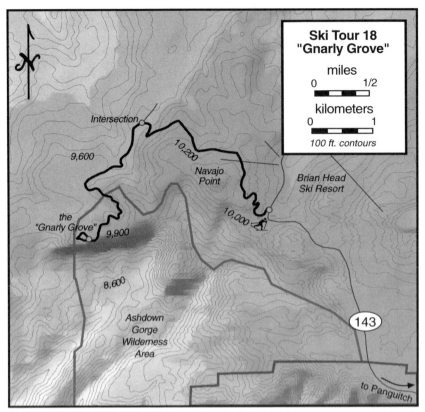

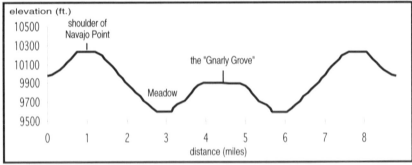

Bristlecone pine trees, a long-lived species that uniquely inhabit the harsh growing conditions near the edges of the Pink Cliffs (Claron Formation). Views into the badlands and cliffs of Ashdown Gorge Wilderness Area.

Other Useful Maps: Dixie National Forest "Travel Map" and U.S. Geological Survey 7.5-minute Quadrangles "Brian Head" and "Flanigan Arch."

Bristlecone pine (*Pinus longaeva*) at Gnarly Grove

How to Get There (Markagunt Plateau Area Map)

See directions for Ski Tour 14—Lightning Point. Use the Lightning Point/Navajo Point winter trailhead and parking area at the sharp bend in the highway.

Ski Tour Description

Although this tour is somewhat long, the treasure at the end is well worth a long day's worth of skiing. Besides the picturesque grove of Bristlecones at the end, the Gnarly Grove tour offers a long but vigorously relaxing trail that passes through groves of fir and spruce. Climbing over the shoulder of Navajo Ridge offers excellent views into the Ashdown Gorge Wilderness Area, Cedar Breaks, and the Great Basin.

The trail starts in a meadow on the west side of the highway, where it takes a sharp bend as noted above. Cross the meadow westward, heading toward Navajo Point, where a skied-in forest road (the Sugarloaf Mountain Road) climbs up to the northeastern shoulder of Navajo Point. At the shoulder point the forest opens up to cat tracks crossing ski runs, and the trail goes under the Navajo lift of Brian Head Resort. Keep following this road as it enters forests, passes through two ravines, and finally arrives at a junction with the Dry Lakes road (see map). Take a left on this road (continuing southwest). Pass through a ravine to a broad, open meadow where Sugarloaf Mountain (a large conical point) is directly visible due west. At the highest point on the ridge upon which this meadow sits, turn a sharp left, leaving the road, but staying along the southern edge of the ridge line. This is a summer hiking trail, which may not be very visible in snow-covered conditions. After about 0.25 mi. (0.4 km.) begins the Ashdown Gorge Wilderness Area, marked by a trailhead sign (which will be snowed over in deep conditions). Beyond this point snowmobiles are no longer permitted. Continue southeast to the base of a sharp ridge, staying along a contour line. Climb slightly southwest along the side of the ridge to its top. Continue through two gullies, to the point where the ridge drops off into the breaks. The Bristlecone forest is visible from quite a distance, and should be a beacon through this unmarked and often untracked portion of this route.

Tour 19: Miller Knoll

Tour Length: 4.3 mi. (6.8 km.) round trip.

Difficulty: Beginner to intermediate backcountry route. Although this tour climbs substantially (600 ft., 180 m. elevation gain), the route follows a graded road surface, and is otherwise an easy tour.

Elevation: 8,480–9,060 ft. (2,580–2,760 m.).

Snow Conditions: Generally snow covered from December to March. Snow conditions can vary greatly annually.

Geological and Other Scenic Features: Excellent views of the Black Rock Desert, an expansive basaltic lava field of Quaternary age. Also, views of Panguitch Lake (to the north), which was formed by the damming of the valley stream by one of these lava flows.

Other Useful Maps: Dixie National Forest "Travel Map" and U.S. Geological Survey 7.5-minute Quadrangle "Panguitch Lake."

How to Get There (Markagunt Plateau Area Map)

From Panguitch, drive west on Utah State Highway 143, just past Panguitch Lake. Two and a quarter miles (3.6 km.) past the Panguitch Lake campground (which is at the west end of the lake) find an

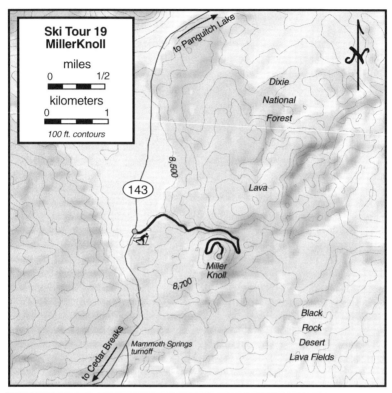

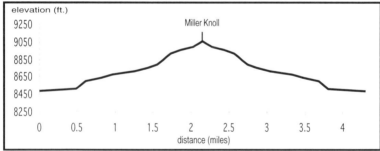

unplowed turnoff for the Miller Knoll Road (marked as Birch Spring Knoll on the highway; to the left). If you reach the turnoff to Mammoth Creek (marked, and also to the left), you've gone too far.

Ski Tour Description

If you're looking for a scenic break from the monotonously red-hued views of the Pink Cliffs around Cedar Breaks, Miller Knoll provides a tour through a very strange and dark landscape. The tour follows an unmarked road to the top of a cinder cone with 180-degree views of black lava.

From the turnoff, follow the road eastward over gently rolling terrain. The lower part of this tour passes over some of the lava flows, often resulting in patchy snow conditions. When the eastern base of the knoll is reached, take a side road that climbs toward a gravel quarry (where the red, cindery rock is usually exposed, even in winter). The road continues switchbacking, and wrapping around the side of the peak, to the views from the top.

Tour 20: Kolob Plateau Overlook

Tour Length: 7.1 mi. (11.4 km.) round trip.

Difficulty: Easier intermediate tour. Although somewhat long, the terrain of this tour is gentle, making it a good long workout for beginner skiers.

Elevation: 8,550–8,900 ft. (2,600–2,710 m.).

Snow Conditions: Generally snow covered from December to March. Snow conditions can vary annually. This route is often tracked by snowmobilers who frequent the Duck Creek Area, often making trailbreaking much easier for skiers.

Geological and Other Scenic Features: Viewpoint of the Pink Cliffs of Eocene Claron Formation, across the Kolob Plateau, down the Virgin River drainage, and into Zion National Park.

Other Useful Maps: Dixie National Forest "Travel Map" and U.S. Geological Survey 7.5-minute Quadrangles "Navajo Lake," "Henrie Knolls," "Strawberry Point," and "Straight Canyon."

How to Get There (Markagunt Plateau Area Map)

The parking area for the Kolob Overlook area is at the turnoff for the Duck Creek Work Camp and Information Center on Highway 14. From Cedar City take Highway 14 past Navajo Lake. The Information Center is opposite the Duck Creek Campground (on the opposite side of Highway 14).

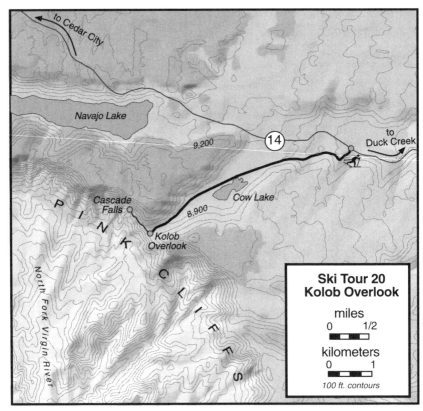

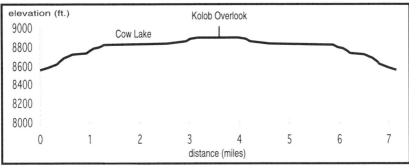

Ski Tour Description

Although generally unknown to skiers, the Duck Creek/Navajo Lake area may be some of the best backcountry touring terrain on the Markagunt Plateau. The scenery is similar to that at Cedar Breaks, with badland exposures of the Pink Cliffs (Claron Formation), forests of Ponderosa pine, fir and spruce, and the curious Bristlecone pine in their usual position at the edge of the Pink Cliffs escarpment.

The trail begins by paralleling the highway along the side of a steep canyon wall, climbing gently to Cow Lake flats. Ski across the flat area, into a deep and narrowing canyon with high plateau surfaces on either side. The dry "lake" can be safely crossed without worry of breaking through the "ice." Follow through this canyon southwest to the plateau escarpment, at the Kolob Plateau overlook.

These deep valleys are the remnants of an ancient drainage system, now cut off by recent emplacement of the lava. One of the more extensive of these lava flows has blocked the former outlet of Navajo Lake, which now sits at the drainage boundary between the Great Basin and Virgin River systems. To the east, Duck Creek flows into the Sevier River, eventually ending at Sevier Lake in western Utah. To the west and south, Navajo Lake begins the Virgin River drainage system, which flows into the Colorado River, eventually ending up in the Gulf of California. Prior to the emplacement of the lava flow, Navajo Lake was part of the Duck Creek/Sevier River system. But now, because the lava has blocked this drainage, the lake's only outlet is via the springs that feed Cascade Falls.

This tour is ideal for snowshoers, the hardiest and most confident of whom may be able to access the side trail to Cascade Falls. This additional route to Cascade Falls is not recommended for skiers, as the trail is carved into the side of the cliff and requires greater stability and downhill control than skis can provide. The water flowing over the falls (greatest in spring) emerges from Navajo Lake by subsurface flow through the soluble limestones of the Claron Formation. Exploration of the cave is not recommended, because the spring water evolves carbon dioxide, an odorless but asphyxiating gas.

Tour 21: Mammoth Cave

Tour Length: 5.0 mi. (8.0 km.) round trip.

Difficulty: Easier beginner route.

Elevation: 7,840–8,000 ft. (2,390–2,440 m.).

Snow Conditions: Most often snow covered from December to March. Because of the low elevation, snow conditions can vary annually, and can be extremely sparse in dry years. This route is often followed by snowmobilers who frequent the Duck Creek Area, providing some "grooming."

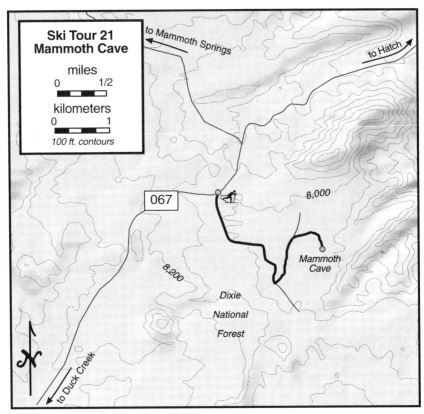

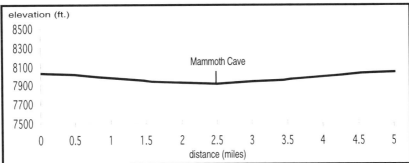

Geological and Other Scenic Features: Mammoth Cave is a lava tube that extends below the surface crust of the lava flow that blankets this portion of the Markagunt Plateau. Much of the forest of this area was burned during the Uinta Flats fire of 1989.

Other Useful Maps: Dixie National Forest "Travel Map" and U.S. Geological Survey 7.5-minute Quadrangles "Henrie Knolls" and "Asay Bench."

How to Get There (Markagunt Plateau Area Map)

The Mammoth Cave tour begins on National Forest Road 067, which is a back road connecting Duck Creek village and the city of Hatch. Note that snow conditions vary on this road, and closures may occur. Check first with the Forest Service office in Cedar City for road conditions. From the Highway 14 area, take the turnoff slightly east of Duck Creek Village. Follow this for 6 mi. (9.6 km.) to a turnoff on the right, marked with a high signpost to Mammoth Cave. If approaching from Hatch on Highway 89, drive 12 mi. (19.2 km.) west on Forest Road 067, to the Mammoth Cave turnoff (marked by a signpost).

Ski Tour Description

Could ski-spelunking be the adventure sport of the new millennium? Have you ever skied to go caving before? Mammoth Cave, a lava tube below the Markagunt Plateau basalt flows, provides such a unique opportunity. Be sure to bring a flashlight for this tour, because the only real scenic highlight is the cave (unless you count a very flat surface covered with a forest recovering from fire).

From the trailhead, follow the snowed-over road surface through the open Ponderosa forest. The amazingly flat surface of this area is formed on a relatively old (vegetated) lava flow, making a somewhat featureless plain, lacking development of a surface drainage network. Continue on the snowed-over road across this plain for 1.4 mi. (2.3 km.) to the first open meadow, where a turnoff (sharp left) is marked by a relatively high signpost to Mammoth Cave. Be sure not to miss it if the sign is snowed over. This second road travels again through the open forest another 0.6 mi. (1 km.) to a right turnoff (also signposted; again may not be visible in excessive snow). This turn is very easy to miss. If you reach another large opening in the forest, you've gone too far. Continue along this road to a sheltered area at the edge of the forest, where the first red rock exposures of the Claron Formation begin. Look closely for the entrance to the cave, which is nothing more than a 30-ft. (10-m.) diameter pit in the ground. You will have to climb over a few boulders in the pit to get to the entrance, which in extremely deep snow (rare at this elevation) may be completely snowed over. Take care in descending into the pit, as the area may be icy. Remember that the cave will be very cold in winter, so be sure to bring extra warm gear.

Tour 22: Markagunt Lava Fields

Tour Length: 2.6 mi. (4.2 km.) round trip.

Difficulty: Easier beginner route. Generally untracked, except when a few snowmobiles have used this trail to access the open country of the surrounding plateau.

Elevation: 9,300–9,340 ft. (2,830–2,850 m.).

Snow Conditions: Most often snow covered between December and March (occasionally from November to May). Conditions may vary greatly annually.

Geological and Other Scenic Features: A chance to explore a very recent (Quaternary) basaltic lava flow.

Other Useful Maps: Dixie National Forest "Travel Map" and U.S. Geological Survey 7.5-minute Quadrangle "Navajo Lake."

How to Get There (Markagunt Plateau Area Map)

The turnoff and parking area for this tour is on the left of Highway 14 (as approaching from Cedar City) about 0.5 mi. (0.8 km.) past the Navajo Lake overlook. If you are approaching from Duck Creek, this is about 0.25 mi. (0.4 km.) past the Navajo Lake campground turnout and snowmobile parking area. A low sign (often snow covered) can sometimes be seen in winter (but is often under deep snow), pointing to the "Lava Beds."

Ski Tour Description

For another unique tour outside of the Cedar Breaks area, the Markagunt Lava area provides an opportunity to explore firsthand some of the basaltic lava that is so often missed when you are whizzing by on the highway. This route provides a short tour to the edge of one of the most recent and most dramatic of these lava fields. Because the snow at these elevations is often rather thin, this is an excellent tour for snowshoers, especially on lightweight model snowshoes. Snowshoers can also easily remove their snowshoes and tromp around the lava boulders in hiking boots.

From the trailhead, ski through the forest to an opening after about 0.4 mi. (0.6 km.). At this point, the trail is marked by orange-flagged posts (for snowmobilers), through the open meadow, and down into a small snow-covered stream, which traces the edge of the lava field (1.3

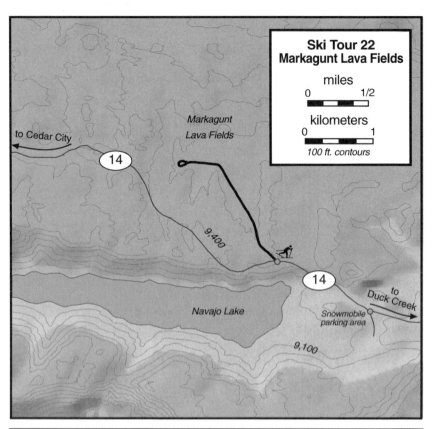

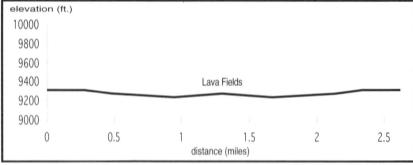

mi., 2.1 km.). The lava is generally not snow covered (except after recent heavy snow), due to the rapid melting of snow on the black rocks, which lack the insulation provided by soil. From this point, one may continue again along the snowmobile route through the forest, or scramble around on some of the boulders. Take care in doing so, as many of the boulders are very loose, due to their very young age, and the lack of soil formation.

Additional Resources:

Brian Head Ski Resort
Reservations, lodging, weather, and ski conditions
P. O. Box 190008
Brian Head, UT 84719
(435) 677-2035
brianhd@mountainwest.net
http://www.brianhead.com

Brian Head Chamber of Commerce
Lodging, businesses, cross-country grooming, local information
1 (888) 677-2810
brianhead@netutah.com
http://www.brianheadutah.com

Inner Harmony Bed and Breakfast
Yurt rental in Brian Head area for cross-country skiers
P. O. Box 87390
Phoenix, AZ 85080
1 (800) 214-0174
http://www.ihretreat.com

Brian Head Sports
Snow conditions, rentals, repairs, etc.
269 S. Highway 143
Brian Head, UT 84719
(435) 677-2014
http://www.brianheadtown.com/bhsports/

Georg's Ski and Bike Shop
Snow conditions, rentals, repairs, etc.
612 S. Highway 143
Brian Head, UT 84719
(435) 677-2013
http://www.brianheadtown.com/Georgs

Cedar Breaks National Monument
National Monument information (closed in winter)
2390 W. Highway 56 Suite 11
Cedar City, UT 84720
(801) 586-9451
http://www.nps.gov/cebr/

Dixie National Forest
Road conditions, weather, campgrounds, permits
USDA Forest Service
Cedar City District
(435) 865-3204
jwhicker@fs.fed.us
http://www.fs.fed.us/outernet/dixie_nf/welcome.htm

AREA 3

The Tushar Range, Including Elk Meadows Ski Area

Mineral Deposits and Stratovolcanoes of the Tushar Mountains

If you were to ask most Wasatch Front skiers to list the highest and most skiable mountain ranges in Utah, most would be completely unaware of the Tushar Range—the little-known giant, just outside of the small town of Beaver, a perfect place for all types of skiing. The Tushars are the third highest mountain range in the state, actually well ahead of the Wasatch Front Range. The tallest peak in the Tushars, Delano Peak, is 12,169 ft. (3,709 m.), putting the Tushars third, behind the Uinta Range and LaSal Mountains of northeastern and southeastern Utah. The elevation of the Wasatch Front Range actually comes in fifth (the highest point is Mount Nebo at 11,928 ft.), behind the Tushars (third) and the Deep Creek Mountains of western Utah (fourth).

At its base elevation of 9,200 ft. (2,800 m.), Elk Meadows Ski Resort (the only downhill resort in the Tushars) often has some of the earliest natural snow of any ski resort in the state. What's more, the resort access highway, Utah State Highway 153, is plowed to elevations of nearly 10,000 ft. in winter, and provides access to much of the skiable terrain in the Tushar high country. Many of the attainable high-elevation peaks in the range (including Delano, Holly, and Belknap) are readily accessible to advanced backcountry skiers. These peaks provide some of the best backcountry downhill runs in the entire western states region. For beginner-to-intermediate ski tourers, the hundreds of square miles of the surrounding high country are also readily accessible for ski touring, accessed via the downhill resort and the surrounding network of Forest Service roads and trails. The staff of the downhill resort also groom a variety of trails for track skiing (both classical and freestyle). For these and many other reasons, the exceptional skiing of the Tushars is truly a little-known Utah gem, well hidden in this easily accessible part of the state. Located about 20 mi. east of the small town of Beaver, just off Interstate 15, the smallish downhill resort of Elk Meadows is unknown to the many tourists who come every year to ski the more widely popularized Wasatch Front.

Serious backcountry and telemark skiers will certainly appreciate the quantities of fresh, light powder that fall every year at Elk Meadows and the surrounding backcountry. Annual snowfall typically exceeds 400 inches per year—some of the driest powder in the state. However, due to its location, high winds blowing out of the west desert often remove most of the snow on the high peaks. Despite this, many sheltered areas in the surrounding highlands are often deep in fresh, dry, and deep powder.

It should be noted that only a few of the Tushar skiing possibilities have been explored in this book; many remain known only to the few who ski this area often. Advanced skiers with backcountry route-finding skills will certainly find the Tushars fruitful for some of the best unknown backcountry in the state. Besides the superb snow and few crowds, the Tushars provide some of the great winter scenery that southwestern Utah is famous for. However, for geological reasons described below, the Tushars are very atypical compared with the red rock scenery that otherwise characterizes the skiable terrain described in this book.

Geology of the Tushar Mountains

The Tushar Mountains and surrounding areas are geologically atypical of the majority of the red rock country described in the rest of this book. The bedrock of the Tushars is almost entirely volcanic, and is therefore generally more subdued in chroma. Being somewhat less expansively stratified than the rocks of the surrounding red rock country, the bedrock of the Tushars does not form expansive plateau surfaces such as those seen on the Markagunt, Paunsagunt, Aquarius, and Boulder Mountain Plateaus in Ski Touring Areas 1, 2, 4, and 5 of this book. There are several reasons for this geological oddity of the Tushar Range.

One thing that stands out in any quick look at a geological map of Utah is the large pink spot that seems to crosscut the patchwork of

Mt. Belknap, Tushar mountains, at alpenglow

patterns typical of the southwestern Utah plateau country (see geology discussion in Ski Touring Area 2 for discussion of the geological history and formation of the plateaus). The pink color of this mapping symbol represents the extensive and thick Tertiary volcanic pile of the Marysvale volcanic province, the largest accumulation of volcanic rocks in the state, centered around the small mining town of Marysvale in Piute County. The 10,000-ft. (3,000-m.) thick volcanic pile in this area is the debris remaining from a large stratovolcano complex that persisted from about 30 to 5 million years ago, but was most active between 30 and 20 million years ago (during the Oligocene to Miocene Periods). The remaining edifices of these stratovolcanos are difficult to identify based on their topographic features, because they have since been eroded and faulted beyond recognition. However, geological mapping and radiometric dating of the bedrock geology have identified several massive ancient calderas that existed at Mount Belknap and Mount Dutton and in Bullion Canyon. The high peaks of the Tushars are generally formed of what remains of the magma chambers that crystallized before being erupted. These rocks are more resistant to erosion than the ash and volcanic fragments deposited in the surrounding areas during eruptions, and they therefore stand out as some of the prominent peaks of the Tushars.

It was during this period of extremely heightened volcanic activity that numerous igneous intrusions (failed eruptions of magma that cooled before being able to reach the surface) produced the abundant hydrothermal alteration of the surrounding bedrock. It is this alteration history that has formed the economic deposits of precious and industrial metals exploited by the mining industry, particularly during the late nineteenth century. Geothermal waters associated with these rising magmas formed mineral deposits of a tremendous variety of precious and industrial metals including gold, silver, lead, copper, mercury, zinc, iron, manganese, uranium, and aluminum and potassium. These last two are found in the Tushars in the form of the curious mineral alunite, which contains appreciable quantities of both aluminum and potassium needed particularly during the wartime emergencies of the twentieth century. The brilliantly colorful results of this mineral alteration can be seen at the "Big Rock Candy Mountain" resort (generally closed in winter), on Highway 89 just north of Marysvale. Here, abundant alteration along veins in the rock, particularly of the mineral Pyrite, has produced an "ice cream sundae" of colored swirls, drips, and oozes, having altered the original bedrock almost beyond recognition. Nearby, at "Lemonade Springs," water emerges with the color and even a slight flavor of lemon, hinting at the alteration minerals contained within (probably Limonite) and the lingering acidity of the mineral-rich groundwater.

Area 3 Ski Tours

Map No.	Ski Tour	Length in mi. (km.)*	Difficulty and Notes*
Elk Meadows Ski Resort Area			
23	Puffer Lake Loop	1.8 mi. (2.9 km.) LP	B
24	Twin Lakes	3.0 mi. (4.8 km.) RT	B (BC, S, T)
25	Cullen Creek Loop	5.7 mi. (9.1 km.) LP	B (BC)
26	Lake Stream	4.9 mi. (7.8 km.) OW	B–I (BC)
27	Skyline Trail Loop	5.5 mi. (8.8 km.) LP	I–A (BC, T)
Three Creeks Area			
28	Three Creeks/Grizzly Ridge	2.4 mi. (3.9 km.) OW	B–I (BC, S, T)
29	The Gorge at Three Creeks	3.8 mi. (6.0 km.) RT	B (BC, S)
30	Strawberry Flats	5.8 mi. (9.2 km.) RT	I (BC, S)
Marysvale Area			
31	Bullion Canyon	3.9 mi. (6.3 km.) RT	B–I (BC, S)

*RT = Round trip; OW = One way; LP = Loop; B = Beginner; I = Intermediate; A = Advanced; BC = Backcountry route, unmarked trail; S = Also recommended for snowshoes; T = Telemark possibilities.

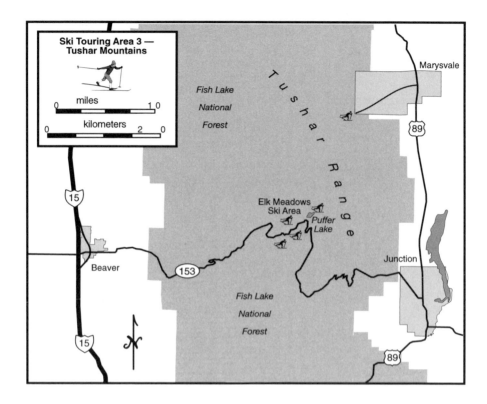

Tour 23: Puffer Lake Loop

Tour Length: 1.8 mi. (2.9 km.) loop.

Difficulty: Easy beginner and first-time skier groomed trail. This is a very short, groomed, flat trail best suited for first-time and beginning skiers. The trails are groomed for both classical and freestyle skiing.

Elevation: All about 9,680 ft. (2,950 m.).

Snow Conditions: Generally some of the best snow in the Tushars. This area is at very high elevation and well sheltered, retaining deep snow between late November and late March, often well into May. The lake is typically frozen solid in the depths of winter, and can be skied across safely. However, if in doubt, check with the ski-grooming staff at Elk Meadows. During late fall and spring, when the lake is soft and the ice thin, your route should follow the lake shore.

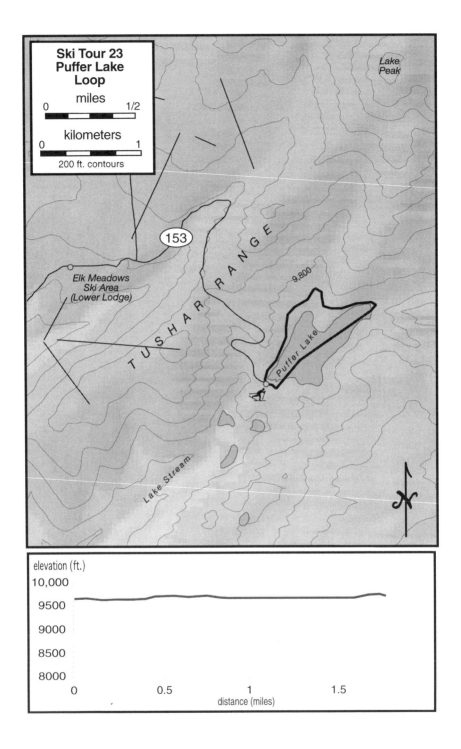

Geological and Other Scenic Features: Puffer Lake, a glacial-dammed lake formed by the terminus of a moraine, a natural dam (but augmented by a man-made earthen dam).

Other Useful Maps: Fishlake National Forest "Travel Map" and U.S. Geological Survey 7.5-minute Quadrangles "Delano Peak" and "Shelly Baldy Peak."

How to Get There (Tushar Mountains Area Map)

From the town of Beaver, just off Interstate 15, take Utah State Highway 153 toward Elk Meadows Ski Resort. Pass the turnoffs to the lower and upper lodges, and continue another 3 mi. (4.8 km.) to Puffer Lake. Use one of the several plowed turnouts nearby, and walk to the road that travels along the west side of the lake.

Ski Tour Description

This short trail traverses a large high-elevation lake in the Tushar high country. It is very short, flat, groomed, and easy to ski in a short amount of time, perfectly suited for first-time skiers. From this loop trail, one may also take off on other, more advanced backcountry trails.

 To follow the groomed trail is easy. The tracks begin by skirting the west side of the lake, climb over a small ridge, and continue to the upper bay. There is a small historic cabin here where the Cullen Creek Road continues up the drainage (see Ski Tour 25—Cullen Creek Loop). The groomed tracks return to the trailhead along the eastern shore of the lake, and in winter conditions cross the lake surface. These trails make for excellent track skiing, and a fun skating loop.

Tour 24: Twin Lakes

Tour Length: 3.0 mi. (4.8 km.) round trip.

Difficulty: Beginner backcountry tour. This is a gentle tour through the woods, and if skied in the most economical way, does not involve any significant climbing ability, especially if following tracks made by well-informed skiers (the resort staff). This route does not follow a summer trail, and there are no trail markings, making backcountry

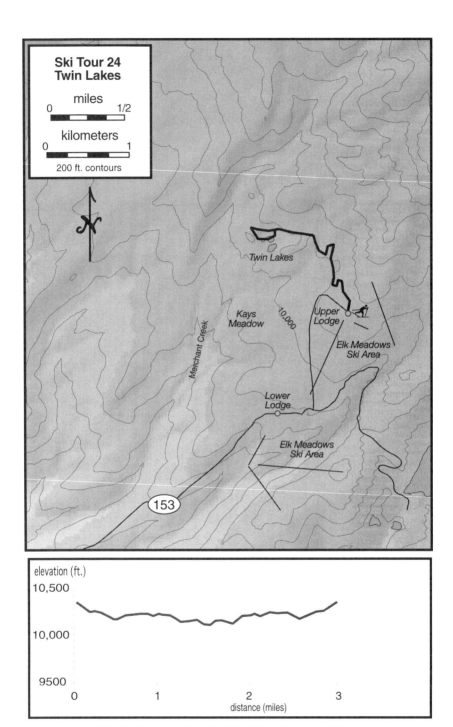

route-finding skills necessary, especially if you are breaking trail. This route is best followed in the tracks of someone who knows the area well.

Elevation: 10,360–10,120 ft. (3,084–3,160 m.).

Snow Conditions: This is a very high-elevation tour with some of the earliest snow in the Tushars. Forested and sheltered conditions also make for excellent backcountry powder. Snow generally persists from late November to early April (at least).

Geological and Other Scenic Features: Nice views of a great deal of the Tushar Mountains region.

Other Useful Maps: Fishlake National Forest "Travel Map" and U.S. Geological Survey 7.5-minute Quadrangle "Shelly Baldy Peak."

How to Get There (Tushar Mountains Area Map)

From the town of Beaver, just off Interstate 15, take Utah State Highway 153 toward Elk Meadows Ski Area. At about 19 mi. (30 km.) is the turnoff to the upper lodge. Park in the large lot and find the trailhead at the northern end of the lot. If necessary, the ski repair and rental staff in the upper lodge can help with trail directions and local conditions.

Ski Tour Description

This short tour is an excellent introduction to the backcountry experience of the Tushars. If marked or skied in, the route is easy to follow, and it provides access to some isolated forests and small meadows with views of the Tushar high country. This short tour also makes for an excellent snowshoe route, by which one can further explore some of the heavily forested areas. From the Twin Lakes area, one can take off on some of the jeep trails and return to the highway via Kay's Meadow, or Merchant Creek. However, this option requires knowledge of the current state of development in the rapidly expanding resort area, and placement of a second vehicle at the base of the trail on Highway 153.

From the parking area, find the backcountry trail heading straight into the woods traveling due north. The resort staff often marks this trail with orange flagging or ski in a set of well-defined touring tracks. The trail descends through open forests to a small, gently sloping meadow. Ski north through this meadow (there are often poles with flagging marking the route across the meadow) to its northern end, where the trail continues west by switchbacking up a small ridge, and then down into a deep gully. After crossing this gully, the trail continues to sidehill through thick aspen forests to a ridge slightly above the Twin Lakes basin. This area is often a playground for snowmobiles, but fresh snow can make for some great telemark play. After looping through the upper lake, the trail returns via the same route.

Tour 25: Cullen Creek Loop

Tour Length: 5.7 mi. (9.1 km.) loop.

Difficulty: More difficult beginner backcountry tour. Although this tour is somewhat long and climbs significantly, the route climbs gently along Forest Service roads, and is very easy to follow.

Elevation: 9,660–10,320 ft. (2,940–3,150 m.).

Snow Conditions: Generally snow covered between late November and late March. Some of the higher elevation meadows and ridges may be windswept and crusty.

Geological and Other Scenic Features: Open meadow and forested country near treeline in the Tushar Mountains highland.

Other Useful Maps: Fishlake National Forest "Travel Map" and U.S. Geological Survey 7.5-minute Quadrangles "Delano Peak" and "Shelly Baldy Peak."

How to Get There (Tushar Mountains Area Map)

The parking and trailhead for this tour are the same as for Ski Tour 23—Puffer Lake Loop (see above for directions).

Ski Tour Description

This tour follows a Forest Service logging road through the country above Puffer Lake. There are excellent views looking north toward the

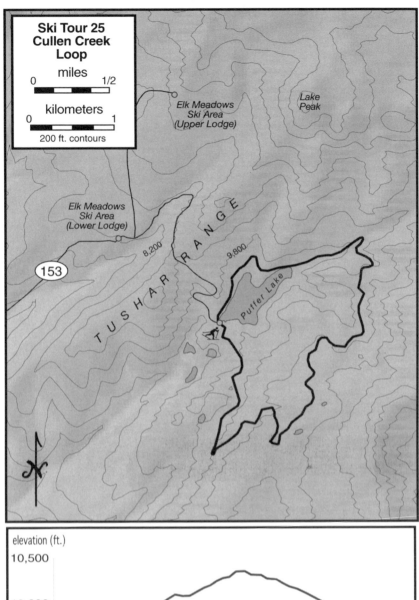
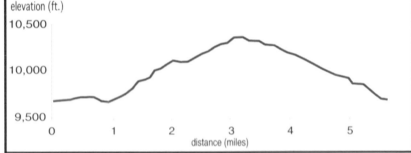

high Tushar peaks, west down the valley, to the west desert and Wheeler Peak, and to Nevada in the far distance.

The route begins by following the groomed Puffer Lake Loop trail (see Ski Tour 23) along the western shore of the lake. The groomed track travels over a low ridge, and begins up the valley at the eastern end of the lake. A small historic cabin is visible at the point where the Cullen Creek trail takes off from the groomed system. Continue up this road about 0.5 mi. (0.8 km) to a sharply ascending turnoff to the right. The main road continues up the creek (the return route of Ski Tour 27—Skyline Trail Loop). After taking this turn, follow the road as it climbs through forests along the side of the ridge. Near the top, the trail opens up into several small meadows with excellent views to the north and west. The trail then drops down to the main highway (which is snowed over at this point) into the beginnings of a broad meadow with heavy snowmobile use (Big Flat). At this point, ski along the snowmobile tracks over the highway surface to the trailhead.

Tour 26: Lake Stream

Tour Length: 4.9 mi. (7.8 km.) one way.

Difficulty: Beginner to intermediate backcountry tour. This route descends gradually along a well-distinguished snowed-over road, and makes for a great fast downhill tour.

Elevation: 8,680–9,660 ft. (2,650–2,940 m.).

Snow Conditions: Generally snow covered between December and March. Some of the south-facing slopes in sunny areas may be slushy or exposed.

Geological and Other Scenic Features: A number of glacial-dammed lakes and up-close views of a very thick ash-flow tuff (volcanic deposit) in the Three Creeks Gorge.

Other Useful Maps: Fishlake National Forest "Travel Map" and U.S. Geological Survey 7.5-minute Quadrangles "Delano Peak" and "Shelly Baldy Peak."

How to Get There (Tushar Mountains Area Map)

The parking area and trailhead for this tour is slightly beyond the Puffer Lake area (see Ski Tour 23—Puffer Lake Loop for directions).

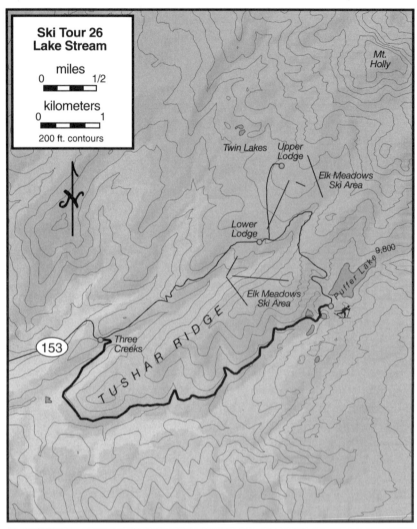

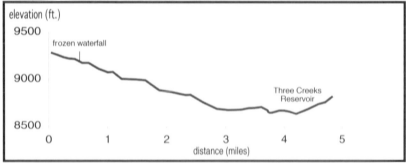

THE TUSHAR RANGE; MINERALS AND VOLCANOES

Continue another 0.25 mi. (0.4 km.) to the end of the plowed road, at which point there are several plowed turnouts for skiers, snowshoers, and snowmobilers. Snowmobiles generally continue up the snowed-over highway toward Big Flat. However, the Lake Stream trail takes off to the right, past a few small cabins into the large drainage. This route is often tracked by snowmobiles, skis, and snowshoes.

If this tour is done as a one-way (as recommended), a shuttle must be arranged, or a second vehicle left at the Three Creeks parking area and trailhead (for directions to Three Creeks, see Ski Tour 28—Three Creeks/Grizzly Ridge).

Ski Tour Description

This tour makes for a fast and fun downhill along the backside of Tushar Ridge. It also passes a scenic frozen waterfall on the back side of a glacial moraine-dammed lake near the top. However, unless a shuttle can be arranged, or a second car left at the endpoint, it is a long uphill back to the trailhead. Check with the staff of the ski resort (at the rental and repair shop of the upper lodge) for possible arrangements of return transportation.

From the trailhead ski down through a series of small glacial moraine-dammed lakes (Blainies, Otter, and Mirror Lakes), past a small summer resort (do not disturb the private property), and continue along the trail to a steep section in the creek where there is a frozen waterfall. From this point, the trail descends along the side of Tushar Ridge through the forested areas, and finally enters an open valley. Keep to the north side of the valley, on the cut road surface (the Paiute ATV trail). At the end of the valley, the ATV trail begins to ascend the slope, just before another branch enters the gorge (see Ski Tour 29—The Gorge at Three Creeks). Either of these trails may be taken toward Three Creeks Reservoir (which is drained). The mapped route follows the upper ATV trail, which continues to wrap around the side of this hill, above the gorge. At the northeast end of the reservoir, the trail climbs up the side of Grizzly Ridge, along a fairly steep grade to the Three Creeks parking area and trailhead (see driving directions above for parking or shuttle arrangements).

Tour 27: Skyline Trail Loop

Tour Length: 5.5 mi. (8.8 km.) loop.

Difficulty: Intermediate to advanced backcountry tour. This route climbs steeply and steadily to a high ridgeline, and requires the greater stamina of confident intermediate to advanced skiers. The route is, however, easy to follow, and passes a cabin at about the mid-point of the climb, perfect for a rest stop.

Elevation: 9,660–11,040 ft. (2,940–3,360 m.).

Snow Conditions: Most often snow covered between late November and early April. The 11,000-ft. (3,350-m.) ridge line may be extremely windswept and barren after windstorms. Snow in the back bowls is generally fresh and light, perfect for telemark fun.

Geological and Other Scenic Features: Expansive views of the entire Tushar Mountain region and beyond, as well as beautiful high-country trails and meadows near treeline.

Other Useful Maps: Fishlake National Forest "Travel Map" and U.S. Geological Survey 7.5-minute Quadrangles "Delano Peak" and "Shelly Baldy Peak."

How to Get There (Tushar Mountains Area Map)

The parking area and trailhead for this tour is at the very tight bend in Highway 153, approximately 0.5 mi. (0.8 km.) past the turnoff to the upper lodge of Elk Meadows Resort (see above tour descriptions for directions to resort). Park in the open shoulder area, and follow the right side of the creek (looking upstream) to a narrow, snowed-over logging road.

Ski Tour Description

The Skyline Trail is one of the most scenic and breathtaking of all trails in the Tushars. The entire length of the trail proper hovers above treeline, crossing the flank of the Tushar Range, and provides some of the most spectacular views of the surrounding area. The ski-touring route described here provides access to the beginning of the Skyline Trail (from which point skiers can access some of the deeper backcountry), then continues down to the Puffer Lake area (see Ski Tours 23 and 25—Puffer Lake Loop and Cullen Creek Loop). From the highpoint of

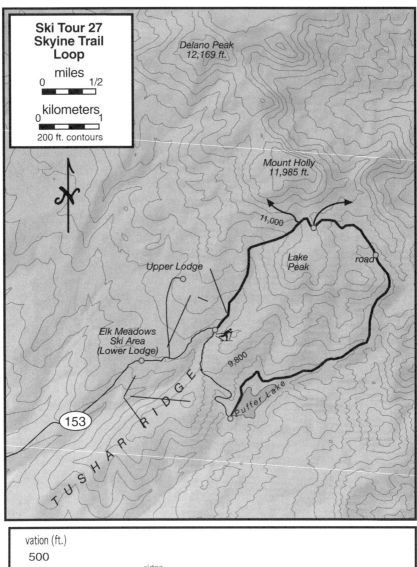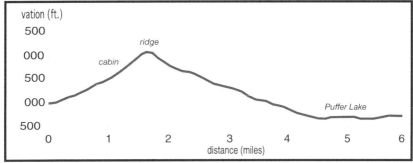

this tour, at a fairly easily attainable ridge at 11,000 ft. (3,350 m.), clear days will provide views of the entire Tushar Mountain region, farther east to the Sevier, Aquarius, Boulder Mountain, and Thousand Lakes Plateaus, and west across the Basin and Range province toward Nevada. Wheeler Peak on the Nevada border is a visible landmark in the west. This ridge is also a good launching point for more advanced skiing to Mount Holly and Delano Peak. These off-trail detours will require more extensive backcountry skills, and under most conditions the use of climbing skins and avalanche equipment.

From the trailhead, follow the stream up through recently cut forests, along the Three Creeks stream. The trail crosses the stream after a short distance, and then follows the left bank of the stream (looking upstream) along a fairly steep grade up to the warming cabin. From this point, continue to climb up the drainage toward the saddle between Mount Holly and Lake Peak. The route becomes steeper, and climbing skins may be useful in some conditions for the final ascent of this ridgeline. However, a few switchbacks will suffice for those with well-tractioned skis. From this ridgeline, advanced skiers may take off toward the north along the Skyline Trail, and toward the ascents of Delano Peak and Mount Holly.

After reaching this ridgeline, the described trail drops off somewhat steeply to the east into a broad meadow. This may be accomplished by switchbacking through the forest, or by way of an open area at the base of Mount Holly. At the southern end of this meadow, the trail catches up with an old logging road, which can be followed in a steady downhill to the Puffer Lake area. From Puffer Lake, one can ski along the road to the beginning of the trail, or leave a second car or arranged shuttle at Puffer Lake, about 1 mi. (1.6 km.) from the trailhead.

Tour 28: Three Creeks/Grizzly Ridge

Tour Length: 2.4 mi. (3.9 km.) one-way.

Difficulty: Beginner to intermediate backcountry tour. This is a gradual downhill trail, generally easy to follow for beginning skiers. Some of the surrounding backcountry terrain makes for suitable detours for intermediate to advanced skiers.

Elevation: 8,400–8,980 ft. (2,560–2,740 m.).

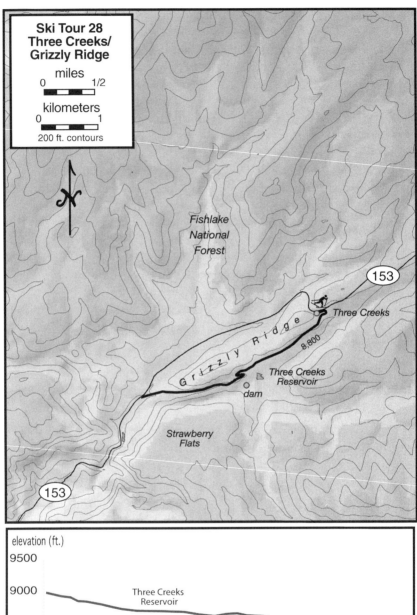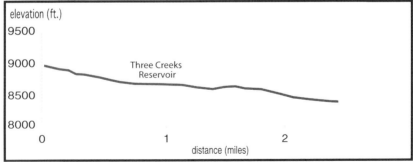

Snow Conditions: Generally snow covered between December and March. Some of the south-facing slopes in sunny areas may be slushy or exposed. However, most of the route is well sheltered and retains snow well.

Geological and Other Scenic Features: Forested country of the Three Creeks drainage area. Often very good wildlife viewing.

Other Useful Maps: Fishlake National Forest "Travel Map" and U.S. Geological Survey 7.5-minute Quadrangle "Shelly Baldy Peak."

How to Get There (Tushar Mountains Area Map)

This tour begins at the Three Creeks Road turnoff, approximately 17 mi. (27 km.) east of the town of Beaver on Utah Highway 153. The Three Creeks area is well marked with a large highway sign and abundant parking (at right) for skiers, snowshoers, and snowmobilers. The ending point of this tour is a small parking area, approximately 2 mi. (3.2 km.) down the road from the Three Creeks parking area. The ending point is marked by an open meadow at the base of Grizzly Ridge, slightly upstream from a small reservoir on the south side of the road. At the upstream end of this meadow is a turnout and parking area to the left, where a vehicle may be left.

Ski Tour Description

This tour follows a Forest Service road around the backside of Grizzly Ridge in the Three Creeks area. Grizzly Ridge is a nicely open forested area, often with nice snow conditions for some quick downhill play. However, the southern slope of the ridge is quite steep and has been avalanche prone in the past, so be sure to be familiar with this potential. Check with the staff at Elk Meadows for details. This tour involves a series of descending switchbacks and the potential for a lot of backcountry exploration, which may also be ideal for snowshoers.

   From the Three Creeks parking area and trailhead, ski down the road/ATV trail to the Three Creeks Valley. The trail follows the north "shore" of the small reservoir, which is drained. Once the earth-fill dam is reached, the trail switches back quickly to the canyon below, which becomes quite deep. The trail then continues downstream, along the southern flank of Grizzly Ridge, to a broad meadow where the road is reached. From this point, one can either return via the same route (a fairly easy ski-out), or leave a second car or shuttle at the trail ending (see directions above for car drop-off point).

Tour 29: The Gorge at Three Creeks

Tour Length: 3.8 mi. (6.0 km.) round trip.

Difficulty: More difficult beginner backcountry tour. This route is generally easy in terms of terrain. However, a few steep sections, and the sometimes dense vegetation in the gorge, may present some difficulty for skiers. Snowshoers will easily overcome these difficulties, making this a good beginner snowshoe route.

Elevation: 8,680–8,980 ft. (2,640–2,740 m.).

Snow Conditions: Generally snow covered between December and March. Some of the south-facing slopes in sunny areas may be slushy or exposed. Snow in the gorge is often deep and very fresh, but willows and a few barbed-wire fences below snow depth can make things somewhat difficult.

Geological and Other Scenic Features: A narrow gorge through a very thick ash-flow tuff (a near-vent volcanic deposit).

Other Useful Maps: Fishlake National Forest "Travel Map" and U.S. Geological Survey 7.5-minute Quadrangle "Shelly Baldy Peak."

How to Get There (Tushar Mountains Area Map)

Use the Three Creeks parking area and trailhead as for Ski Tour 28—Three Creeks/Grizzly Ridge.

Ski Tour Description

The gorge at Three Creeks is a narrow canyon that cuts through very thick ash-flow tuff (volcanic deposit), with striking bedrock walls. This tuff is a major geological unit in the Tushar Mountains, which defines much of the shape of the Tushar high country. In this area, one can trace many of the flat surfaces that are defined by the top of this erosionally resistant unit throughout the Tushars (see, for example, Ski Tour 30—Strawberry Flats). This tour is a great way to see some of the local geological features and perhaps observe some of the wildlife that frequents this area. Besides being a great ski tour, this trail is excellent for snowshoers.

From the Three Creeks parking area and trailhead, ski down the road toward Three Creeks Reservoir. At the tip of the reservoir (which is drained), drop off the main road and ski alongside the "shoreline"

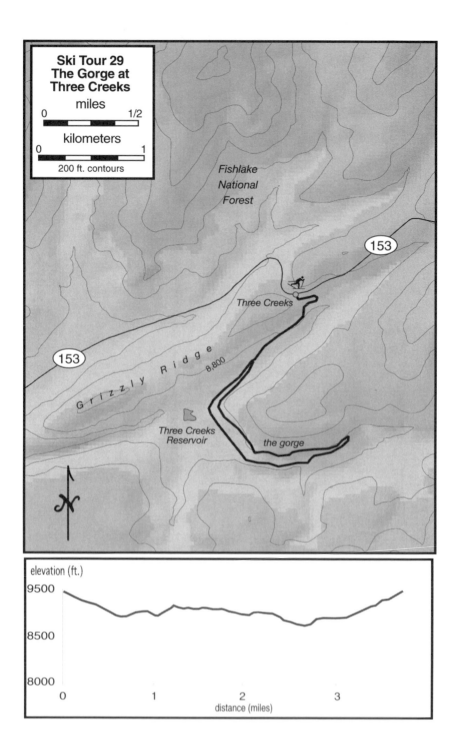

The gorge at Three Creeks

wrapping around the hill below the road surface. There is a nice wave-cut bench formed by this shoreline that makes for a good skiing surface. Once you reach the center of the reservoir area, the gorge is visible straight ahead. Several spots in the gorge may provide some difficulty for skiers due to thick willows and a couple of barbed-wire fences. However, continue through the gorge, until an ATV trail (typically used by snowmobilers in winter) is reached. Follow this trail northward, up a sidehill to the main road surface. The road may then be followed, above the gorge, in return to the reservoir tip and finally to the trailhead via the same route.

Tour 30: Strawberry Flats

Tour Length: 5.8 mi. (9.2 km.) round trip.

Difficulty: Intermediate backcountry tour. Most of this tour traverses very easy terrain. However, the final ascent to the flats involves a steep road climb, and may require good traction and the climbing skills of the more seasoned intermediate backcountry skier.

Elevation: 8,680–9,120 ft. (2,640–2,780 m.).

Snow Conditions: Generally snow covered between December and March. Some of the south-facing slopes in sunny areas may be slushy or exposed. Strawberry Flats is covered in well-packed snow crust, especially in spring.

Geological and Other Scenic Features: Excellent views back at the Tushar Mountain high country.

Other Useful Maps: Fishlake National Forest "Travel Map" and U.S. Geological Survey 7.5-minute Quadrangle "Shelly Baldy Peak."

How to Get There (Tushar Mountains Area Map)

Use the Three Creeks parking area and trailhead as for Ski Tour 28—Three Creeks/Grizzly Ridge.

Ski Tour Description

Strawberry Flats is a broad meadow area, which is formed by the upper surface of the erosionally resistant volcanic bedrock layer seen in Ski Tour 29—The Gorge at Three Creeks. Similar flat surfaces can be traced throughout the Tushars, at this general elevation, sloping down toward the valleys below in a broad arch. The flats make for nice spring-crust skiing and a playground for touring around. The views at the edge are also spectacular, with all of the Tushar peaks laid out on the horizon. This tour also makes for a good snowshoe route, especially for overnight trips into the secluded Strawberry Flats area.

    From the Three Creeks parking area and trailhead, ski down the road surface until the Three Creeks Reservoir basin is reached. The trail follows the road along the north side of the drained reservoir, and crosses the dam at its end. Once the dam is crossed, the trail begins to climb several steep grades through the forests toward the flats. The final ascent along the road is fairly steep and can be icy and somewhat difficult if heavily tracked by snowmobiles. At the south end of the meadow

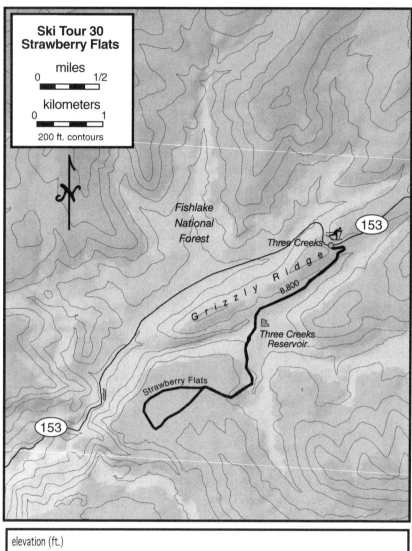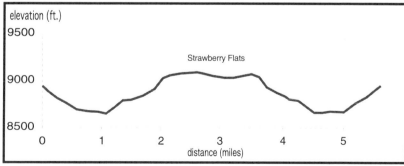

is a Boy Scout camp, which is private property and should not be disturbed. The Boy Scouts do occasionally take winter trips to this camp, which can make the place somewhat crowded. After playing in the flats, and enjoying the views (which are spectacular during alpenglow), the tour returns to the trailhead via the same route.

Tour 31: Bullion Canyon

Tour Length: 3.9 mi. (6.3 km.) round trip.

Difficulty: More difficult beginner to intermediate backcountry tour. In most fresh snow conditions, this tour can be very easy. However, if the road becomes icy with vehicle use, the grade can be quite steep and require the use of downhill abilities, and is best done with metal-edged skis.

Elevation: 7,320–8,400 ft. (2,230–2,560 m.).

Snow Conditions: Snow conditions vary greatly with temperature, but the area is generally skiable from December to March. In this steep canyon, north-facing slopes are well sheltered. However, a few sunny spots on south-facing slopes are often bare or rocky. Snow on road surfaces is often tracked by vehicles or ATVs.

Geological and Other Scenic Features: Two very photogenic frozen waterfalls, as well as many historical remnants of the Marysvale mining district.

Other Useful Maps: Fishlake National Forest "Travel Map" and U.S. Geological Survey 7.5-minute Quadrangle "Mount Brigham."

How to Get There (Tushar Mountains Area Map)

This tour is accessed from the small town of Marysvale, on U.S. Highway 89. From the highway, at the corner of Main and Center, turn west toward Bullion Road, which travels due west, at first through town. At the outskirts, this road branches to the left and continues by winding past large and small cabins spread out along the road up Bullion Canyon. The road is generally plowed to the Marysvale corporate boundary and the beginning of Forest Service property, which is marked by the beginning of the Canyon of Gold Driving Tour (with a

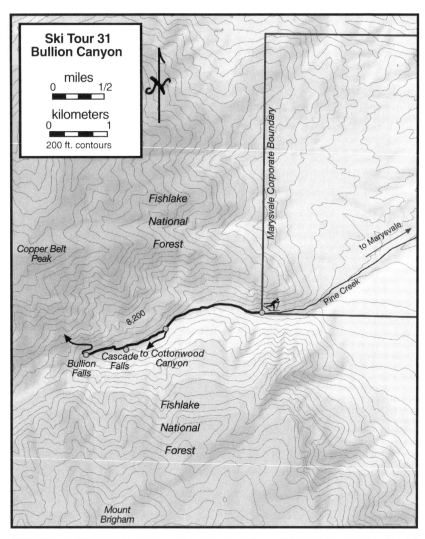

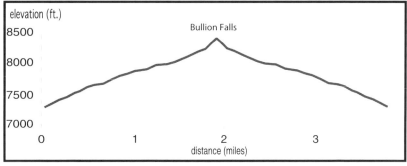

Bullion Falls on the
Bullion Canyon Trail

narrow-gage railway car sign). Drive up the canyon to this point, or as far as you are able, and park in an acceptable spot to begin the tour. Along the narrow road, there are several turnouts with space for parking. However, the road is narrow, and a turnout should be used so as not to disturb traffic. Even the upper road surface is often tracked by vehicles and ATVs, so it is sometimes better to drive farther than the marked trailhead at the Forest Service boundary.

Ski Tour Description

This tour provides an opportunity to see some of the remains of the local mining history of the Tushar mining days, which began furiously in the late 1800s and continue to today in a very limited way. There are remains of several old cabins, a mill, and other miscellaneous mining debris remaining all along the route. A tour guidebook is available at the trailhead, with detailed historical information on all of the stops on the road/hiking tour. Besides the mining history, the trail follows a beautiful narrow, glacially eroded canyon, cut into the volcanic rocks that typify the Tushars. At the end point of the tour are two frozen waterfalls, which make for a nice view and are popular among ice climbers. Because of the steep grades and narrow trails, this route is also very good for snowshoers.

From the appropriate parking area, ski up-canyon along the steeply graded and narrow road surface until a bridge marking Bullion Village is reached. At this point the road crosses the bridge and continues along the left bank of the stream (looking upstream), but the ski/snowshoe trail continues along the right bank (marked by a signpost to Bullion Falls). This trail continues along the side of the hill to two frozen waterfalls (Cascade and Bullion Falls). Both of these falls cascade over the erosionally resistant volcanic ash-flow tuff layer seen as prominent cliffs throughout the Tushar Range (see Ski Tours 29 and 30—The Gorge at Three Creeks and Strawberry Flats). This tour may also be a way for advanced skiers to access some of the deeper backcountry via the trail that continues above the falls and the Cottonwood Canyon road on the north side. However, the intermediate tour of the map returns down-canyon via the same route.

Additional Resources:

Elk Meadows Ski Resort
Trail grooming, rentals, repairs, local conditions
P. O. Box 511
Beaver, UT 84713
1 (888) 881-7669
(435) 438-5433
http://www.elkmeadows.com
information@elkmeadows.com

Fish Lake National Forest
Road conditions, weather, campgrounds, permits
Beaver Ranger District
P. O. Box E
575 S. Main St.
Beaver, UT 84713
(435) 438-2436
http://www.fs.fed.us/r4/fishlake/index.html

Tushar Mountain Tours
Yurt rental and guided ski tours in Big John Flat area
P. O. Box 1193
Beaver, UT 84713
(435) 438-6191
twomilehigh99@yahoo.com

AREA 4

The High Plateau Country from Boulder to Torrey

Pleistocene Ice Caps of the Aquarius, Table Cliffs, and Boulder Mountain Plateaus

The high plateau country of the Aquarius, Table Cliffs, and Boulder Mountain Plateaus has been appropriately called the "throne of the Colorado Plateau," and it is truly one of Utah's finest untapped resources for all kinds of winter sports, especially ski touring and snowshoeing. Although skiing and snowshoeing are fairly familiar winter sports in many of the other areas described in this book, this somewhat remote region remarkably sees only a few skiers and snowshoers annually. This fact is very ironic, because some of the best skiable terrain in southern Utah, especially during spring, is to be found on these high-elevation snow-capped plateaus.

The Boulder, Aquarius, and Table Cliffs Plateaus are the highest red rock plateau surfaces in North America, and are more of a connected system than isolated plateaus. Boulder Mountain is an upper step (hightop), towering above the more extensive Aquarius and Table Cliffs Plateaus, which some consider a single surface. The highest point on the Boulder Mountain Hightop is 11,328 ft. (3,452 m.) at Bluebell Knoll, while most of the surrounding dozens of square kilometers of plateau surface are above 11,000 ft. (3,350 m.). The adjacent Aquarius and Table Cliffs Plateaus are slightly lower, both at about 10,400 ft. (3,170 m.), and very easily attainable on skis or snowshoes, especially during spring, after formation of the "spring crust." The open meadow country of these high plateau surfaces is especially beautiful and serene when snow covered, when broad expanses of flat white extend for miles and miles upon end. The plateau surfaces are a great playland for skinny

127

skating skis, especially after formation of the spring crust. This hard surface, best in the early morning, makes for extremely fast skiing across long distances of the expansive high country, well beyond the intermediate tours described here.

Because of its isolation and relatively infrequent ski traffic, the high plateau surfaces of this region can be reached only by traversing somewhat long distances. There are no paved or plowed roads that access the upper plateaus until very late spring, when the snow has melted. The closest winter-plowed highway over these high plateaus is Utah State Highway 12, between Torrey and Boulder Town, which traverses only the shoulder of the Boulder Mountain Hightop. Basic winter travel services are available in the surrounding towns. However, the exception is skiing-specific services such as repair, rental, and guide services. Despite this relative inaccessibility, the western part of this area (Aquarius and Table Cliffs Plateaus in Ski Tours 36, 37, and 38) is actually very close to Bryce Canyon National Park and Ruby's Inn (see Touring Area 1 for details).

Other gravel Forest Service roads traverse the plateau region and may serve as additional access points for further exploration beyond the scope of this book. The tours described in this section begin from the most readily accessible roads, such as Highway 12, over the eastern shoulder of Boulder Mountain, and Highway 22 between Bryce Canyon and Antimony. Further winter exploration of the high plateau country is possible via other less accessible routes such as the Hell's Backbone and Posey Lake roads, especially if four-wheel drive is available.

Skiers of the high plateaus region should be especially prepared for any type of ski emergency, or prepared to travel much greater distances back to repair or rental shops. For its inaccessibility and remoteness, much of the Boulder, Aquarius, and Table Cliffs Plateaus is really most appropriate for intermediate to advanced skiers who are well prepared and familiar both with backcountry skiing and with this area—or at least accompanied by those with such experience. It should be noted that many of the beginner-to-intermediate tours described here might be viewed as general guides to areas for advanced skiers' further exploration into the depths of the untracked backcountry of the high plateaus.

Geology of the High Plateaus

Boulder Mountain derives its name from the underlying volcanic bedrock, which often leaves behind large boulders strewn across the

Ski touring atop the 11,000-foot Boulder Mountain Plateau

more stable plateau surfaces. The Boulder Hightop is entirely circumscribed by a steep cliff (up to 600 ft., 200 m. high) formed of this volcanic bedrock, making access to the hightop somewhat difficult. The ring of cliffs is surrounded by a variety of Late Pleistocene surficial features closely associated with ice-age glaciations.

Although the bedrock of the high plateaus region consists of the volcanic debris from the Marysvale Volcanic Province (see Ski Touring Area 3), perhaps the most interesting aspect of the geological history of the high plateaus occurred during the Pleistocene, when a massive ice sheet sat atop the Boulder Mountain Hightop Plateau. Two types of glacial features belie the ice-age history of this region. First, there are glacially associated features found on the hightop surface, most of which are inaccessible to winter travelers due to snow cover. Patterned ground, evidence of the action of permafrost, which has expanded and contracted the soil into patterned blocks, can be observed in several places on the hightop, especially near Bluebell Knoll. Other features on the bedrock surface of the plateau include striations, glacial erratics, rock glaciers, and glacial drift. Glacial striations are deep grooves cut into the bedrock underlying the flowing ice, carved by rocks entrained in the glacial flow. Erratics are large blocks of bedrock, seemingly out of place, which could only have been carried by the flow of ice. Rock glaciers and glacial drift are two very distinctive types of surficial deposits, always associated with glaciated regions.

Abundant evidence of the Pleistocene glaciation is also evident in some of the elongate valleys that extend radially from the hightop surface, where fingers of ice called outlet glaciers extended from the hightop ice cap. Within these valleys are a number of glacial moraines, the deposits formed by melting of tongues of the main glacier flowing from the plateau, down the valleys, finally depositing the coarse and poorly sorted rock at its end. Glacial topography is particularly well developed at Pleasant Creek, where glaciers extended down the valley as far as 6,600 ft. (2,010 m.) elevation. Such ice-sheet glaciers atop extensive plateau surfaces are relatively rare in the modern glacial world. The only similar modern plateau ice caps are observed in the Conger Range on Ellesmere Island, northern Canada, which serve as the most suitable analog to the ancient environment of the Boulder Mountain Hightop ice sheet.

Beyond the morainal deposits of the valleys, the plateau margins are also characterized by massive landslide deposits, many of which are several square miles in extent. These areas are characterized by hummocky, irregular topography, small marshy areas, and often by aspen forests, which are more suited to the disturbed conditions. The landslides are more prominent on the north and east slopes of the plateau, and are particularly well observed in the Singletree Creek area. The potential causes of these ancient landslides are many. The volcanic rock underlying the plateau is predominantly volcanic tuff, which weathers easily to sticky clays, well suited to slipping along failure planes. However, the extreme activity during the Pleistocene has since reduced (a few of the ancient slides are partially active). The Pleistocene activity was probably enhanced by increased meltwater from the ice cap and glaciers, frost action of cooler temperature, and swelling of clay minerals in the wetter environment of the ice ages.

At only 600 ft. (200 m.) lower in elevation, the conjoined Aquarius and Table Cliffs Plateaus show no evidence of Pleistocene glaciation. This attests to the fact that these high elevations are on the brink of glaciation. During the most recent ice age, the lowest-elevation glacial ice straddled the boundary between these two areas at somewhere between 10,400 and 11,000 ft. (3,170–3,350 m.). As a general rule southern Utah mountains and plateaus above 11,000 ft. were glaciated during the Pleistocene, while lower elevation regions were not. Furthermore, during winters as late as the early twentieth century, snow fields in open areas atop Boulder Mountain persisted well into the month of August.

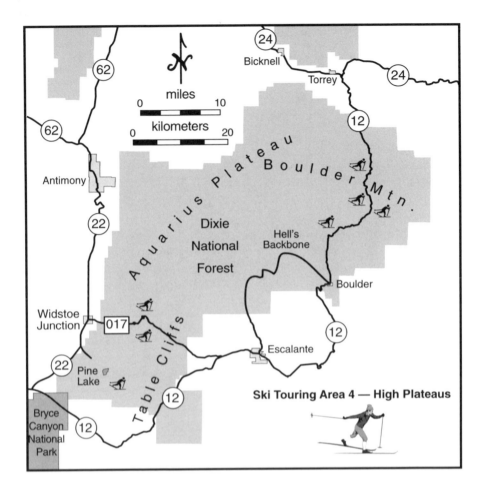

Area 4 Ski Tours

Map No.	Ski Tour	Length in mi.(km.)*	Difficulty and Notes*
Boulder Mountain Plateau			
32	Oak Creek Reservoir	5.9 mi. (9.4 km.) RT	B (BC)
33	Wildcat Pasture Loop	2.4 mi. (3.8 km.) LP	B (BC, S)
34	Steep Creek Lake	5.7 mi.(9.1 km.) RT	I (BC, S, T)
35	Happy Valley	5.8 mi. (9.3 km.) RT	I (BC, S)
Aquarius/Table Cliffs Plateaus			
36	Barney Top	8.8 mi. (14.0 km.) RT	I (BC)
37	Griffin Top	12.0 mi. (19.2 km.) RT	A (BC)
38	Pine Lake/Henderson Canyon	18.0 mi.(28.8 km.) RT	I–A (BC)

*RT = Round trip; LP = Loop; B = Beginner; I = Intermediate; A = Advanced;
BC = Backcountry route, unmarked trail; S = Also recommended for snowshoes;
T = Telemark possibilities.

Tour 32: Oak Creek Reservoir

Tour Length: 5.9 mi. (9.4 km.) round trip.

Difficulty: More difficult beginner backcountry tour. The touring route follows a Forest Service road and is therefore easy to follow and gentle in its climb. However, the nearly 1,200 ft. (370 m.) of steady climbing and extended length of this tour will test the stamina of skiers of beginning abilities. The return will require some familiarity with downhill skiing techniques for skinny skis.

Elevation: 8,860–10,040 ft. (2,645–3,060 m.).

Snow Conditions: Although snow may be somewhat scarce at times at the trailhead, snow depths increase rapidly with elevation. The upper plateau is generally snow covered from late November to April, and often well into May, depending on snowfall during winter.

Geological and Other Scenic Features: Open meadow country of the Boulder Mountain region. Further extensions to the Boulder Mountain Hightop.

Other Useful Maps: Dixie National Forest "Travel Map" and U.S. Geological Survey 7.5-minute Quadrangle "Lower Bowns Reservoir."

How to Get There (High Plateaus Area Map)

This tour, and all of those in the Boulder Mountain area (Ski Tours 32–35), are accessed via scenic Utah State Highway 12. To get to the Oak Creek trailhead from the town of Boulder in the south, travel north on Highway 12 about 21.5 mi. (34.4 km.) to the Oak Creek Reservoir turnoff (at left). Or, from the town of Torrey in the north, travel south on Highway 12 about 20.5 mi. (32.8 km.) to the Oak Creek turnoff, which is about 0.5 mi. (0.8 km.) past Pleasant Creek Campground. At right, there is a small plowed parking area for winter recreation, at which the trailhead starts.

Ski Tour Description

This tour is a great way to climb up into the Boulder Mountain high country near the plateau's high surface. The trail begins at relatively high elevation and travels to a scenic lake basin in the cirque of an ancient glacier that has carved its way into the eastern edge of Boulder Mountain. For advanced skiers going farther to the plateau surface,

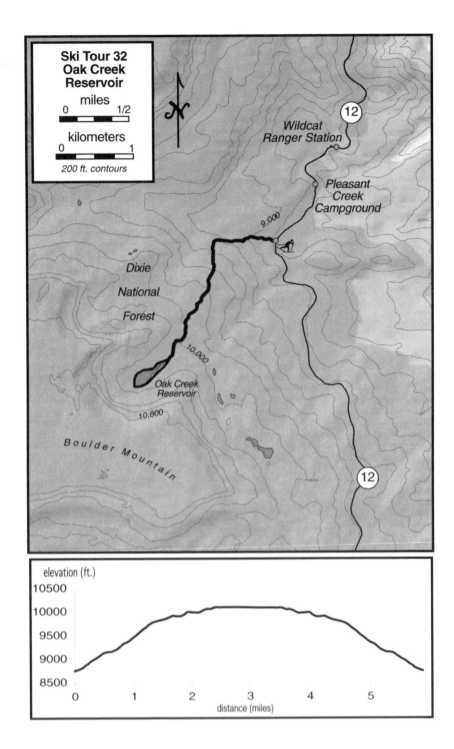

this is a great access point from an already high elevation along Highway 12.

From the parking area, the tour follows the relatively steep but steadily climbing Forest Service road, winding its way through spruce and aspen forests, and a few open meadows, to a ledge upon which a number of small lakes and reservoirs sit at the base of the Boulder Mountain cliffs. This area may be fruitful for further exploration, especially around the meadow and lake country, or via the steeper trail toward the hightop surface. If going toward the plateau, be prepared for another 800-ft. elevation gain, on steep grades, that will likely require climbing skins, avalanche awareness, and more stamina. The described beginner route returns to the trailhead via the same trail.

Tour 33: Wildcat Pasture Loop

Tour Length: 2.4 mi. (3.8 km.) loop.

Difficulty: Easy beginner backcountry tour. This is a great tour for beginner and even for strong first-time skiers to get out into the backcountry of the Boulder Mountain area. However, some familiarity with backcountry skiing techniques will be required or acquired on this tour.

Elevation: 8,720–8,940 ft. (2,660–2,720 m.).

Snow Conditions: Generally snow covered from December to March. The trail through this meadow area is generally well sheltered, and at this high elevation it retains snow well. Snow season is generally from December to late March.

Geological and Other Scenic Features: Very good for wildlife viewing.

Other Useful Maps: Dixie National Forest "Travel Map" and U.S. Geological Survey 7.5-minute Quadrangle "Lower Bowns Reservoir."

How to Get There (High Plateaus Area Map)

This tour is accessed via scenic Utah State Highway 12. From the town of Boulder in the south, travel north on this highway about 22.5 mi. (34.2 km.) to the Paradise Creek trailhead on the left, about 0.5 mi. (0.8 km.) past Pleasant Creek Campground. From the town of Torrey

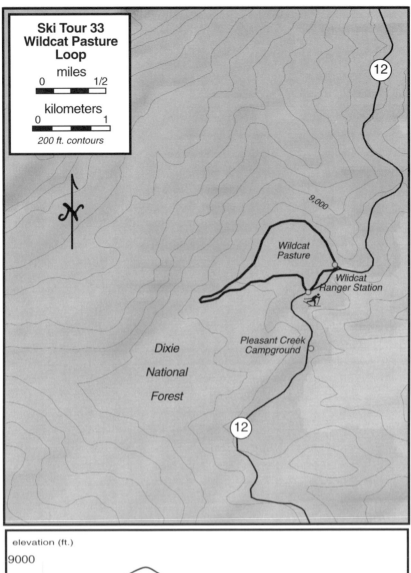
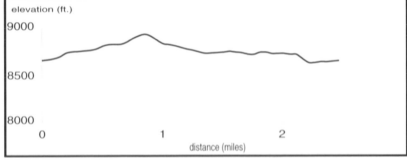

in the north, travel south on Highway 12 about 20.5 mi. (32.8 km.), where the Paradise Creek trailhead turnoff is at the right. There is a small plowed parking area for winter recreation, at which the trail starts.

Ski Tour Description

This is a very easy tour, through some open meadows and large aspen forests of the Boulder Mountain high country. The trail stays in the flat lowlands in the bottom of one of the more extensively glaciated valleys extending from the hightop. It is a good introduction to a backcountry skiing experience in this remote and untracked region, with very little risk or equipment requirements. The snow can be deep at times, and if you are skiing after a recent snowstorm, be prepared for some difficult trailbreaking. This tour is often good for snowshoers, who may be advised to use larger model snowshoes during the deep snow conditions that frequently occur.

From the Pleasant Creek trailhead, ski slightly north, on the marked trail through the forested area. The trail is marked through the forest with Forest Service tree blazes and is relatively easy to follow. The trail then shortly emerges into the pasture area, where, if tracks are not already set, the route may be difficult to follow. However, if you stay at the south end of the pasture, climbing over low hills through some of the fringes of the forest, the trail continues up-canyon to the end of the flat pasture area. From this point, the tour reverses direction, and follows the north perimeter of the pasture, back to the Wildcat Ranger Station area (unoccupied in winter). From the guard station, continue to ski through the most open and easily skied area in return to the Pleasant Creek trailhead.

Tour 34: Steep Creek Lake

Tour Length: 5.7 mi. (9.1 km.) round trip.

Difficulty: Intermediate backcountry tour. A fair amount of climbing, a few steep sections, and the overall length make this tour a challenge for those of intermediate skiing skills.

Elevation: 9,600–10,080 ft. (2,920–3,070 m.).

Snow Conditions: Some of the best snow along the Highway 12 area.

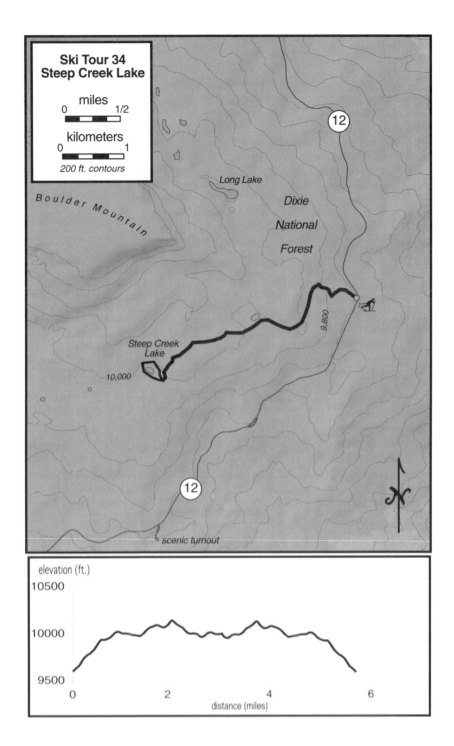

Coyote tracks in crust on Boulder Mountain

At this high elevation, snow is generally retained well into spring. However, during storms, high winds through the pass can remove snow in some of the open areas and make for crusty conditions in the meadows at the beginning of the trail. During major winter storms, this area also is highly prone to white-out conditions. Shortly after snowstorms, trail-breaking can be difficult due to overly abundant snowfall.

Geological and Other Scenic Features: Open meadows and forests of the Boulder Mountain Region.

Other Useful Maps: Dixie National Forest "Travel Map" and U.S. Geological Survey 7.5-minute Quadrangles "Lower Bowns Reservoir" and "Deer Creek Lake."

How to Get There (High Plateaus Area Map)

This tour is accessed via scenic Utah State Highway 12. From the town of Boulder in the south, travel north on this highway about 19.5 mi. (31.2 km.) to the Steep Creek Lake trailhead, at left, about 2 mi. (3.2 km.) past a scenic turnout on the right. Or, from the town of Torrey in the north, travel south on Highway 12 about 22.5 mi. (36 km.), where the turnoff is at the right. This will be about 2.5 mi. (4 km.) past Pleasant Creek Campground, a local landmark. There is a small plowed parking area for winter recreation, at which the trail starts.

Ski Tour Description

This tour provides access to some of the very beautiful open meadows and lake country on the south slopes of the Boulder Mountain Hightop. The area is great for wildlife viewing and the simple experience of the expansive and seemingly endless terrain. The meadows interlace with thick forest of quaking aspen and Engelmann spruce. This open, rolling meadow country is ideal for beginning telemark skiers wanting to practice a few turns. Snowshoers will also appreciate this tour, and its potential for further exploration into the backcountry and wildlife viewing. Larger model snowshoes are advised when snow conditions are deep. The trail begins near the top of the pass along Highway 12, and is one of the best launching points for advanced skiers to access the upper surface of the Boulder Mountain Hightop.

From the Steep Creek trailhead, follow the snowed-over Forest Service road as it climbs steeply at first, quickly reaching some of the open meadow and rolling hill country spotted with small lakes. The road then continues through a series of ups and downs, with a final descent down into the most sizable of the surrounding small lake basins—Steep Creek Lake. At this point, the main tour returns via the same route, although there are many other possibilities for detours in the surrounding backcountry.

Tour 35: Happy Valley

Tour Length: 5.8 mi. (9.3 km.) round trip.

Difficulty: Intermediate backcountry tour. A fast downhill, sometimes questionable snow conditions, and the overall length make this tour appropriate for the intermediate skier.

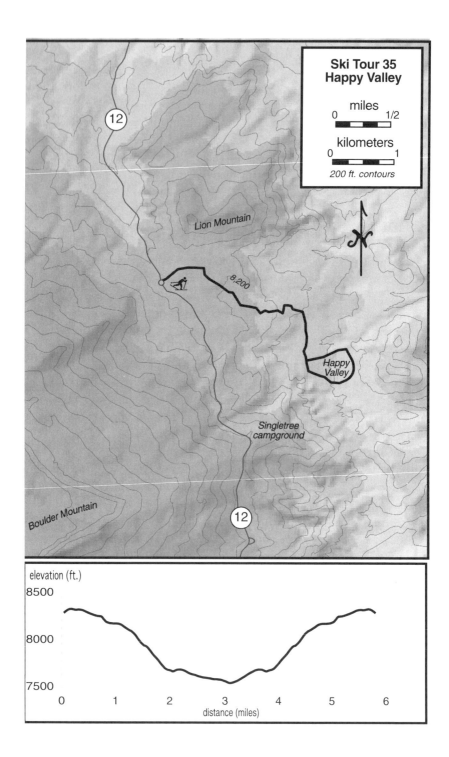

Elevation: 8,240–7,540 ft. (2,510–2,300 m.).

Snow Conditions: Snow can be somewhat spotty at these low elevations, and is best after a fresh snowfall from a winter storm. The trail is generally snow covered from late December to March. In spring of high-snowfall years, the meadows are great for "spring crust" skiing.

Geological and Other Scenic Features: Views off toward large-scale geological features such as the Henry Mountain laccoliths, the Circle Cliffs, and Waterpocket Fold of Capitol Reef National Park.

Other Useful Maps: Dixie National Forest "Travel Map" and U.S. Geological Survey 7.5-minute Quadrangles "Lower Bowns Reservoir" and "Grover."

How to Get There (High Plateaus Area Map)

This tour is accessed via scenic Utah State Highway 12. From the town of Torrey in the north, travel south on Highway 12 about 17 mi. (27.2 km.), where the turnoff to Happy Valley is at the left. Or, from the town of Boulder in the south, travel north on this highway about 19.5 mi. (31.2 km.) to the trailhead, at right, about 1.5 mi. (2.4 km.) past Singletree Campground on the right. There is a small plowed parking area for winter recreation, at which the trailhead starts.

Ski Tour Description

This tour descends off the shoulder of the Boulder Mountain Highway to a pleasant little valley with occasional views off into Capitol Reef National Park to the east. From these points, one can view large-scale geological features such as the Henry Mountain laccoliths, the Circle Cliffs, and Waterpocket Fold. The steep descent and sometimes patchy snow at these lower elevations make this tour also ideal for snowshoers.

From the Happy Valley trailhead, ski through the open meadow country following the road surface toward the wooded areas. Once the forests begin, the trail begins to descend rather sharply, with occasional nice views off to the east. At the base of a large hill is Happy Valley, a nicely enclosed meadow. After skiing around the meadow, the tour returns to the trailhead via the same route.

Tour 36: Barney Top

Tour Length: 8.8 mi. (14.0 km.) round trip.

Difficulty: More difficult intermediate backcountry tour. This tour is quite long, and climbs significantly, although the skiing is relatively easy.

Elevation: 9,280–10,440 ft. (2,830–3,200 m.).

Snow Conditions: Snow at this elevation is very abundant and reliable, especially in winter. The access road may be snowed over at significantly lower elevation during winter. Spring is the best time to ski, as snow level is rising to nearly 9,000 ft., and a good spring crust forms. Check with the local Forest Service ranger district for road, weather, and snow conditions.

Geological and Other Scenic Features: Unique views from the very high elevation Table Cliffs Plateau. Beautiful parkland country of the hightop.

Other Useful Maps: Dixie National Forest "Travel Map" and U.S. Geological Survey 7.5-minute Quadrangles "Griffin Point," "Pine Lake," and "Sweetwater Creek."

How to Get There (High Plateaus Area Map)

This tour is accessed via Forest Service Road 017, which traverses the Escalante Mountains between Widstoe Junction and Escalante. From Highway 12 on the west side (near Bryce Canyon National Park and Ruby's Inn), take Highway 22 north from its intersection with Highway 12 (turning north at the junction toward Antimony, at the intersection where Highway 63 leads south toward Bryce Canyon). Travel 13 mi. (21 km.) to Widstoe Junction, where there is a signpost marking a turnoff to the right toward Escalante (Forest Service Road 017). Travel on this road as far as snow permits, to the pass if possible. At the pass, the trails to Barney and Griffin Tops begin.

The second access route from Escalante begins about 5 mi. (8 km.) west of Escalante, and 20 mi. (32 km.) east of Henrieville (also on Forest Service Road 017, marked with a signpost toward Widstoe Junction). This route approaches the trailheads from the opposite direction, through the same pass as that described above. The shared trailhead for both Barney Top (to the south) and Griffin Top (to the north) is at the high pass on this gravel Forest Service road. Signposts mark both of these routes, which may potentially be driven slightly farther during high snowline conditions.

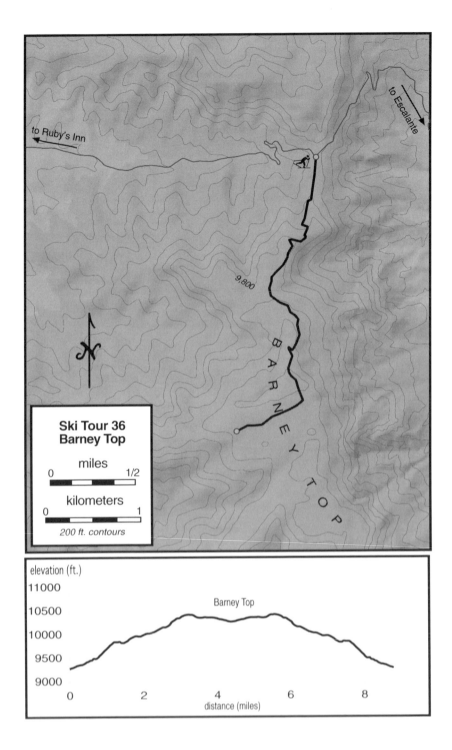

THE HIGH PLATEAUS; PLEISTOCENE ICE CAPS

Ski Tour Description

This tour provides a great opportunity to experience the backcountry of the Table Cliffs area, a unique experience for those who have seen these massive cliffs looming on the horizon in the distance from the rim at Bryce Canyon. This tour is most easily accessible in late spring, when the road to the pass is snow-free to higher elevation, and when a good spring crust has formed. A few snowmobilers traverse this route to the trail across the Aquarius Plateau, and are generally not bothersome. In some cases, the few snowmobile tracks up the road make for a much easier access to the hightop flat country.

From the trailhead at the pass, ski along the narrow rim traversing the neck of the Table Cliffs. This wide-open road climbs steadily, with views alternating between the east and the west. Once the trail travels over a broad hill and begins to descend, the Barney Top surface broadens out, with views to either side. From this point one can explore further the extensive plains of the upper plateau surfaces, with excellent views down into the Grand Staircase–Escalante region. Prominent landmarks include "The Blues," an amphitheater of blue Cretaceous claystones, the Paunsagunt Plateau and Bryce Canyon, the Straight Cliffs, and Navajo Mountain in the distance.

Tour 37: Griffin Top

Tour Length: 12.0 mi. (19.2 km.) round trip.

Difficulty: This is a very long tour requiring a steady climb of nearly 1,200 ft. (370 m.) at least, and will challenge the stamina of even more advanced backcountry skiers.

Elevation: 9,280–10,480 ft. (2,830–3,200 m.).

Snow Conditions: Snow at this elevation is very abundant and reliable, especially in winter and early spring. The access road may be snowed over at significantly lower elevation during winter, especially following recent snowfall. Spring is the best time to ski, as snow level rises to near 9,000 ft. and a good spring crust forms. Check with the local Forest Service ranger district for road, weather, and snow conditions.

Geological and Other Scenic Features: Unique views from the very high elevation Table Cliffs Plateau. Beautiful parkland country of the hightop.

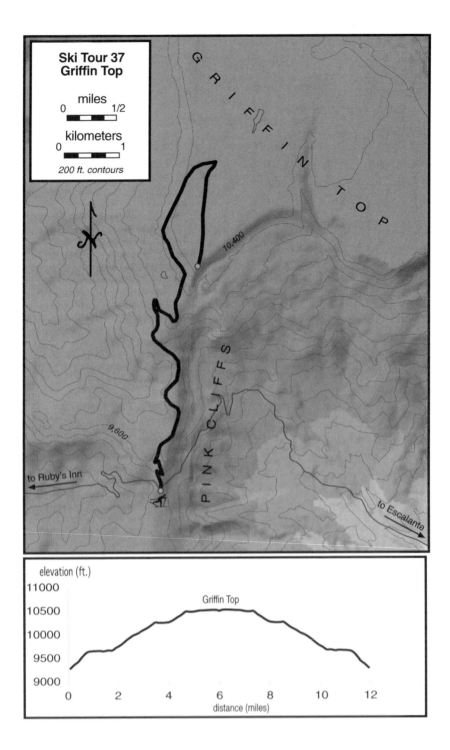

Other Useful Maps: Dixie National Forest "Travel Map" and U.S. Geological Survey 7.5-minute Quadrangles "Barker Reservoir," "Pine Lake," "Grass Lakes," and "Griffin Point."

How to Get There (High Plateaus Area Map)

See directions for Ski Tour 37—Barney Top. The Griffin Top tour uses the same access road (Forest Service Road 017).

Ski Tour Description

Griffin Top is the southernmost extent of the massive Aquarius Plateau that is the backbone of the high plateaus region. Much of the Aquarius Plateau is relatively inaccessible for day-trip ski tours due to excessive distances from plowed highways. One of the best access points to the plateau is the Forest Service road between Widstoe Junction and Escalante, which goes over the broad pass between Griffin Top and Barney Top described above. This is the route used by snowmobilers to access the 40 mi. of the Great Western trail, which traverses the desolate Aquarius. For very hardy ski tourers, this climb is accessible, and the reward of the plateau skiing on the surface is well worth any effort in climbing at least 1,200 ft. A few snowmobile tracks often make trail-breaking on this access road much easier. Furthermore, once the plateau is reached, skiers can easily get away from the potential impact of snowmobile use. This pass is also a great launching point for extended overnight tours deep into the high country of the "throne of the Colorado Plateau."

From the trailhead area, ski along the Griffin Top road, generally due north, climbing steadily toward the plateau surface. Once you reach Griffin Top, the expansiveness is truly amazing, with almost 360-degree views of pure, white meadows covered in snow. If a good crust has formed, these surfaces can be skied for miles, very quickly. Even freestyle skiing is possible in some conditions. This snowed-over access road is really the only practical way to the top of the Aquarius, so the return route follows the same route back to the trailhead.

Tour 38: Pine Lake/Henderson Canyon

Tour Length: 18.0 mi. (28.8 km.) round trip.

Difficulty: Depending on the length of snow cover on the Pine Lake Road, this tour can range from intermediate to advanced skills. If the snow begins at the highway, this tour will require the strength and stamina of very advanced skiers (1,340 ft., 410 m. elevation gain). However, if the snow line is near Pine Lake, as in early winter or late spring, the trail is appropriate for intermediate skiers (600 ft., 200 m. elevation gain from Pine Lake to the overlook).

Elevation: 7,540–8,880 ft. (2,300–2,710 m.).

Snow Conditions: Snow can be somewhat spotty at this elevation, even in winter. During heavy snow years, the Pine Lake road may be snowed over down to the highway. Spring is the best time to ski, as snow level rises to near Pine Lake, and a good spring crust forms. Check with the local Forest Service ranger district for road, weather, and snow conditions to Pine Lake campground, probably the best launching point for this tour.

Geological and Other Scenic Features: Views of the Eocene Claron Formation exposed in the Table Cliffs. Expansive views into the Grand Staircase region to the south.

Other Useful Maps: Dixie National Forest "Travel Map" and U.S. Geological Survey 7.5-minute Quadrangle "Pine Lake."

How to Get There (High Plateaus Area Map)

This tour is accessed via Utah State Highway 22 between Bryce Canyon and the town of Antimony. From the junction with Highway 12, near Bryce Canyon and Ruby's Inn, take Highway 22 north toward Antimony. Travel 11 mi. (17.6 km.) to the Pine Lake road (Forest Service Road 122), marked by a signpost to Pine Lake and Powell Point. Drive as far up the road as snow permits (snow may extend as far down as the highway).

Ski Tour Description

This area provides some truly spectacular and unique views of the Table Cliffs area. From the Henderson Canyon overlook, one has up-close and personal views of the Table Cliffs (Pink Cliffs of the Eocene Claron

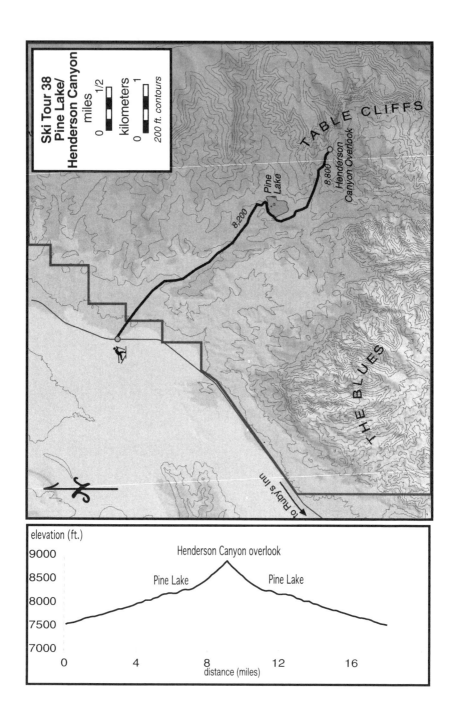

Formation), with variously colored cliffs and badlands of the Grand Staircase–Escalante National Monument in the distance. Although the tour is somewhat long, and almost inaccessible in winter, this route may be shortened significantly when snow lines are higher by driving farther up the Pine Lake road. From Pine Lake itself, the Henderson Canyon overlook is very easily attainable, especially during spring. This is definitely the best part of the tour (between Pine Lake and the overlook), and is even worth the potential trudge up the somewhat barren road to Pine Lake.

From Highway 22, drive as far as you are able toward Pine Lake. If necessary, ski on the road surface to the Pine Lake turnoff (just before reaching the campground). Ski around the north shore of the lake, along the surface of the augmentation dam. The trail then wraps back up onto the road that climbs through meadow and sagebrush country up a broad gully, traveling generally east. This road continues up to an edge near the high cliffs, from which one can look down to the south into the Grand Staircase region. There are also abundant contorted Bristlecone pines in their typical location at the edge of the Pink Cliff exposures.

Additional Resources:

Dixie National Forest (Teasdale and Escalante Ranger Districts)
Local conditions, trails, roads, campgrounds, etc.

Teasdale Ranger District (for Boulder Mountain area)
138 E. Main St.
P. O. Box 90
Teasdale, UT 84773
(435) 425-3702
wjeffrey@fs.fed.us
http://www.fs.fed.us/dxnf/d5_main.html

Escalante Ranger District (for Table Cliffs
  and Aquarius Plateau areas)
755 W. Main St.
P. O. Box 246
Escalante, UT 84726
(435) 826-5403
fwilson@fs.fed.us
http://www.fs.fed.us/dxnf/d4_main.html

AREA 5

The Fish Lake National Forest Area Near Richfield
Tectonics and Faults on the Fish Lake Plateau

The Fish Lake area is another fine example of an extremely skiable high-country plateau that simply has not been developed or pursued to any extent for cross-country skiing or snowshoeing. Although snowmobiling truly reigns supreme as the winter sport in central Utah, there is certainly great potential for further "multiple-use" activities such as ski touring and snowshoeing out of the Fish Lake National Recreation Area and surrounding highlands.

Fish Lake sits at nearly 9,000 ft. (2,740 m.), elevation and receives good quantities of fine, dry snow. The surrounding hightop plateau areas range up to 11,600 ft. (3,540 m.), and retain a great deal of snow well into late spring, great for skiing the spring crust. Most of the beginner to intermediate tours described in this section traverse some of the beautiful quaking aspen (*Populus tremuloides*) and even sagebrush (*Artemisia tridentata*) country surrounding Fish Lake and Johnson Valley Reservoir. Two of the more advanced tours ascend through spruce (*Picea engelmanni*), Subalpine fir (*Abies labiocarpa*) and aspen forests to the surrounding high country above treeline (see Ski Tours 42 and 43 —The Craters and Fish Lake Hightop). These peaks provide expansive views of the surrounding region, particularly across some of the other connected high plateaus, such as Thousand Lakes Mountain, the Boulder Mountain, Aquarius, and Awapa Plateaus (see Ski Touring Area 4), and as far as the Tushar Range to the southwest (Ski Touring Area 3).

The Fish Lake National Recreation Area, surrounding Fish Lake, is very accessible from the Sevier and Sanpete Valleys, which contain the country towns of Salina, Sigurd, Richfield, Joseph, and Monroe (see Fish Lake Area Map). A short climb up the plateau toward Loa leads to the turnoff toward Fish Lake within the Fishlake National Forest. Most of the facilities, including the resort sites, cabins, and campgrounds, are entirely closed in winter. But the area is still very popular, particularly on weekends, among local anglers, sportsmen, and snowmobilers. The Fish Lake access highway (Utah Highway 25) is plowed at least as far as the Bowery Haven resort, providing access to the trails described in this section.

Geology of the Fish Lake Plateau

The bedrock that underlies the Fish Lake Hightop Plateau is geologically connected with the more extensive lava flows that underlie the Boulder Mountain Hightop and Thousand Lakes Mountain to the south and east. These extensive surfaces, now highly uplifted, were until very recently a connected flat and low-lying region across which the massive lava flows spread out from the Marysvale Volcanic Province (see Ski Touring Area 3 for description of the geology of this extensive volcanic region). Since that time (the Oligocene to Miocene), the lithospheric crust of this region has been uplifted to a surface elevation as great as 11,000 ft. (3,350 m.), and torn apart by the extensional tectonic setting that characterizes the Basin and Range Tectonic Province.

The Fish Lake area presents some of the best evidence for the continuing and active development of the Basin and Range, as it slowly usurps the Colorado Plateaus. The lake itself sits within a graben basin, a narrow, elongate trough between the mountain ranges on either side (horsts of Fishlake Hightop and Mytoge Mountain). The bottom of the elongate basin is dropping with respect to the mountains due to extensional tectonics of the surrounding landscape. As the Basin and Range expands as a result of deeper plate tectonic forces, the landscape compensates by extending. In doing so, new sedimentary basins are formed between north-south trending mountain ranges. This type of topography characterizes the Basin and Range, which is famous for endless north-south elongate mountain ranges floating in an ocean of sedimentary basins, like battleships aligned at sea. Small, saline lakes characterize this region, most of them having no outlet to the Pacific Ocean. The Colorado Plateaus, on the other hand, are tectonically stable and are characterized by high plateaus with continuous surfaces of similar underlying bedrock, being slowly eroded by the downcutting of the Colorado River.

The Fish Lake graben presently sits in the precarious position at the active boundary between these two tectonic and physiographic provinces—the Basin and Range Province to the west and the Colorado Plateaus region to the east. While the Basin and Range Province continues to show abundant tectonic activity, especially at its eastern margins, the Colorado Plateaus are generally stable, with old, inactive fault systems. This very important transition zone between two vastly different landscapes has been a strong influence on the recent tectonic evolution of the western United States, and has been called "the Wasatch Line." The Wasatch Line is a major zone of weakness in Earth's crust, roughly dividing the state into its eastern and western portions, and has been demonstrated to be actively migrating eastward. As this migration proceeds, the Basin and Range slowly dices up the Colorado Plateau with individual earthquake movements along the major north-south-trending faults, which become progressively younger eastward. The Fish Lake graben itself is some of the most recent evidence of this eastward migration. The full development of the basin has not yet proceeded to the point that Fish Lake is like the other closed-basin, saline lakes of the Basin and Range, such as the Great Salt Lake. Rather, it is currently captured in its earliest stages of development, still a high-altitude freshwater lake with an outlet to the Colorado River, via Johnson Reservoir and the Fremont River. As the basin continues to develop, the drainage of Fish Lake will eventually be usurped by the closed Great Basin system to the west, and Fish Lake will eventually become yet another of the many closed basin lakes, assuming that the present condition of the Basin and Range–Colorado Plateaus transition continues.

Evidence of this change in drainage patterns is documented by the local geology and paleohydrology of Fish Lake. This high-elevation lake basin sits atop a wobbly drainage divide, wobbling between its northern outlet to the Colorado River eventually ending in the Pacific and its southern outlet to the Sevier River, which eventually drains into salty Sevier Lake in western Utah. An ancient stream bed has been identified, showing past drainage via the southern outlet, which is now 50 ft. (15 m.) higher than the current northern outlet to the Fremont and Colorado. Evidently the southern outlet has very recently been abandoned as the northern section of the basin has dropped more quickly than the southern portion, sending the lake's overflow through the northern outlet to the Colorado. As this active basin continues to develop and subside on geological time scales, this drainage-basin wobbling will likely continue, eventually resulting in a basin similar to the older and more developed systems such as the Sevier and Sanpete Valleys to the west. A new basin will develop to the east, and again usurp more of the Colorado River's precious water.

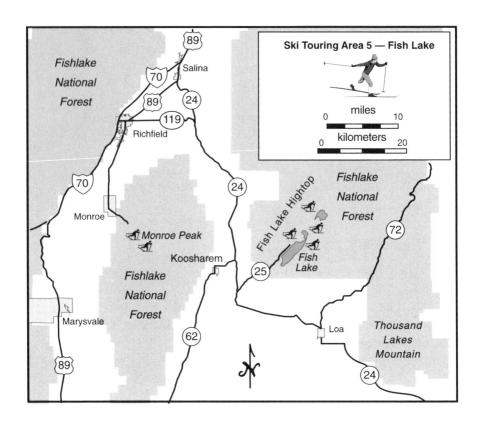

Area 5 Ski Tours

Map No.	Ski Tour	Length in mi. (km.)*	Difficulty and Notes*
Fish Lake Area			
39	Johnson Valley Reservoir	15.2 mi. (24.3 km.) RT	B–I
40	Porcupine Draw Loop	11.0 mi. (17.6 km.) LP	I (BC, S)
41	Lakeshore	5.1 mi. (8.2 km.) RT	B (S)
42	The Craters	11.6 mi. (18.5 km.) RT	A (BC, S)
43	Fish Lake Hightop	10.9 mi. (17.5 km.) RT	A (BC, S)
44	Pelican Point Overlook	3.6 mi. (5.7 km.) LP	B (BC, S)
Other Areas			
45	Monroe Peak	23.9 mi. (38.3 km.) RT	I–A (BC, T)

*RT = Round trip; LP = Loop; B = Beginner; I = Intermediate; A = Advanced;
 BC = Backcountry route, unmarked trail; S = Also recommended for snowshoers;
 T = Telemark possibilities.

Tour 39: Johnson Valley Reservoir

Tour Length: 15.2 mi. (24.3 km.) round trip.

Difficulty: More difficult beginner to intermediate tour, depending on distance. The elevation gain of this tour is minimal, but the distance can be long. However, during low snow conditions of early winter and late spring, one may drive significantly farther up the route, making this tour much shorter. At times, and especially with four-wheel drive, one can drive as far as the shore of Johnson Valley Reservoir, making this a very easy ski tour around the shores of the lake. Route finding is extremely easy, as this tour follows the snowed-over highway grade.

Elevation: 8,860–9,000 ft. (2,700–2,740 m.).

Snow Conditions: Snow conditions vary greatly between years. Generally skiable from December to March. Due to exposure, snow in some spots on the road can be spotty and slushy in spring. Heavy snowmobile use along the Fish Lake Highway is common.

Geological and Other Scenic Features: Nice overview of the Fish Lake valley, Johnson Valley Reservoir, and Fish Lake itself.

Other Useful Maps: Fishlake National Forest "Travel Map" and U.S. Geological Survey 7.5-minute Quadrangle "Fish Lake."

How to Get There (Fish Lake Area Map)

The parking area and trailhead for this, and for all of the ski tours in the Fish Lake area, is at the end of plowing on Utah State Highway 25 (Fish Lake access highway). During the depths of winter, this is typically at the Bowery Haven resort, which is the location of the trailheads marked on the following maps. However, during low-snow years, and in early winter and spring, one may drive farther up this highway toward Pelican Point, Widgeon Bay, and Johnson Valley Reservoir. To get to Fish Lake from the north, exit the combined Interstate 70/U.S. 89 highway (between Salina and Richfield) using exit 48 to Utah Highway 24 toward Sigurd, Fish Lake, and Loa. If coming from Richfield, access Highway 24 by taking the East Glenwood cutoff road (Utah Highway 119), from the turnoff on Highway 89 through town. Highway 24 climbs steeply up the plateau, near the peak of which is the turnoff for Highway 25 toward Fish Lake. Drive to the end of the plowed road for skiing access.

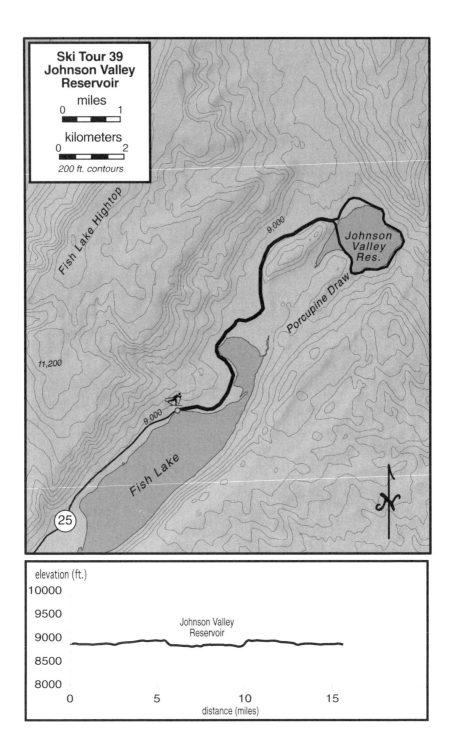

Johnson Valley Reservoir

Ski Tour Description

This is a very easy road tour, with nice views of the Fish Lake graben area. It travels down into a secluded little valley and around the shores of Johnson Valley Reservoir, which is generally at very low water level in winter.

From the parking area at the end of plowing (generally near the Bowery Haven resort), ski along the snowed-over highway that follows near the shoreline around Pelican Point, continues past Widgeon Bay, and begins to descend a small canyon down toward Johnson Valley Reservoir. This small storage reservoir is actually lower in elevation than Fish Lake, and is a good example of the realignment of the surface drainage patterns in the active tectonic setting of the Fish Lake hightop graben. The tour around the secluded reservoir valley is a good escape from the snowmobile trail that follows the road, which is especially active on weekends. A short trip up Porcupine Draw from the reservoir (see also Ski Tour 40—Porcupine Draw) is also well worth the effort.

Tour 40: Porcupine Draw Loop

Tour Length: 11.0 mi. (17.6 km.) loop.

Difficulty: Easier intermediate backcountry tour. Although the climbing is generally gentle, some narrow and steep sections of trail and the long distance present the most difficult challenges on this tour. However, if you can drive to the Widgeon Bay Lakeshore trailhead, the trail is significantly shorter.

Elevation: 8,860–9,040 ft. (2,700–2,760 m.).

Snow Conditions: Generally skiable from December to March. Snow along the shore of the reservoir may be somewhat spotty due to exposure and high winds.

Geological and Other Scenic Features: Secluded valleys and thick forests.

Other Useful Maps: Fishlake National Forest "Travel Map" and U.S. Geological Survey 7.5-minute Quadrangle "Fish Lake."

How to Get There (Fish Lake Area Map)

The parking area and trailhead for this, and for all of the ski tours in the Fish Lake area, is at the end of plowing on Utah State Highway 25 (Fish Lake access highway). See more detailed directions under Ski Tour 39—Johnson Valley Reservoir.

Ski Tour Description

The secluded trail through Porcupine Draw and Lake Creek are an excellent way to escape some of the weekend snowmobile traffic at Fish Lake, while still enjoying the relatively accessible backcountry areas. Because of a few narrow and steep sections of trail, and the frequent need to bushwhack through scrubby aspen and even sagebrush, this tour is often best done on snowshoes, especially if snow conditions are spotty or icy.

The tour begins by following the snowmobile tracks over the snow-covered highway, beginning at the end of plowing (typically at the Bowery Haven resort, or farther up if possible). The road and snowmobile trail follow the shore of the lake around Pelican Point and Widgeon Bay to the Lake Creek access to the Lakeshore Trail. This point is marked by a trailhead signpost that descends down to several

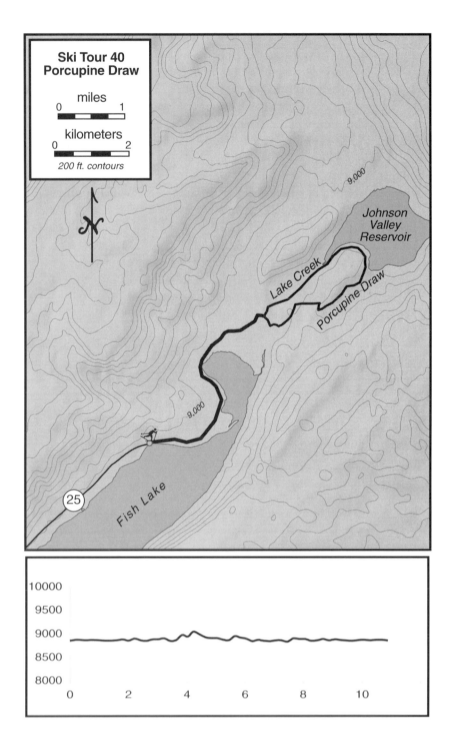

interpretive signs, just above the swampy stream area. From this trailhead, take the trail toward the "Craters," skiing south at first. At this point, the Porcupine Draw trail quickly splits off by climbing to the northeast up a broad sagebrush-covered gully to a low ridge. Once the top of the ridge is reached, the trail enters a forest of aspens with a few scattered spruce. The trail then follows a jeep trail through a gully and up over another small ridge, finally descending into the open areas of Porcupine Draw. Ski down this secluded valley to Johnson Valley Reservoir. Ski along the southern shore of the reservoir, wrapping around a rocky ridge, where a large number of boulders are strewn along the shoreline. This shoreline then leads into a canyon of Lake Creek, the stream that enters Johnson Valley Reservoir from Fish Lake. Within this canyon, the route meets back up with the shoreline trail, visible within the open country. Follow the creek and trail through the marshy areas back toward the trailhead, after which the tour returns along the road and snowmobile trail to the parking area.

Tour 41: Lakeshore

Tour Length: 5.1 mi. (8.2 km.) round trip.

Difficulty: A very easy beginner ski tour. The terrain is very flat (staying along the shore of Fish Lake), and the route is easy to follow and relatively short.

Elevation: 8,860–8,880 ft. (2,700–2,710 m.).

Snow Conditions: Snow conditions vary greatly between years. Generally skiable from late December to March. Barren conditions may exist during dry years, especially in sunny areas.

Geological and Other Scenic Features: Nice overview of the Fish Lake valley.

Other Useful Maps: Fishlake National Forest "Travel Map" and U.S. Geological Survey 7.5-minute Quadrangle "Fish Lake."

How to Get There (Fish Lake Area Map)

The parking area and trailhead for this, and for all of the ski tours in the Fish Lake area, is at the end of plowing on Utah State Highway 25 (Fish Lake access highway). See more detailed directions under Ski Tour 39—Johnson Valley Reservoir.

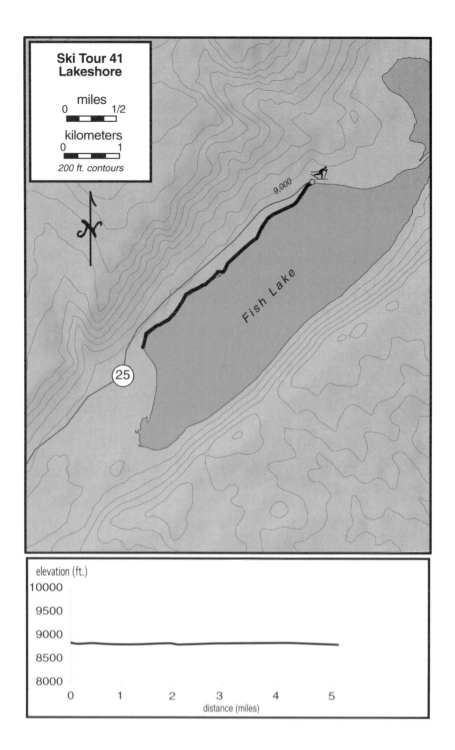

Ski Tour Description

This is a very easy ski touring trail, which simply follows the shore of Fish Lake along the summer-marked Shoreline Trail. The tour provides a variety of views and historical interpretive signs. The trail may be continued beyond the mapped endpoint through some of the campgrounds and ice-fishing areas popular at the south end of the lake. This tour also offers a quick tromp through the snow on snowshoes. Often, during thin snow conditions, the lightweight racing variety suffice.

This segment of the Lakeshore Trail begins at the Bowery Haven trail access (typically at the end of plowing on the highway). From this point, descend down to the trail, which simply follows the lakeshore, sometimes along berms lined with planted rows of aspens. The trail passes several campgrounds and resort areas and a number of interpretive signs, finally ending at Doctor Creek campground. From this campground, there is a plowed road used by ice fishermen to access the southern shore of the lake, a trip alongside of which may make for a nice detour. The tour returns to Bowery Haven via the same route.

Tour 42: The Craters

Tour Length: 11.6 mi. (18.5 km.) round trip.

Difficulty: Advanced backcountry tour. The steep uphill section to the hightop surface and the overall elevation gain will require the stamina and skill of advanced skiers. Climbing skins may be required or useful in some conditions. However, the steep ascent is much more manageable on snowshoes, making this an easy but long intermediate snowshoe tour.

Elevation: 8,860–9,660 ft. (2,700–2,940 m.).

Snow Conditions: Snow conditions vary significantly between years. This tour is generally skiable from December to March. Due to exposure, snow in some spots on the Fish Lake Highway to the Lake Stream trailhead can be spotty and slushy in spring. Heavy snowmobile use along the Fish Lake Highway section of trail is common. Although the climb is significant, this tour is ideal for snowshoers, particularly due to the steep climb up to the plateau surface.

Geological and Other Scenic Features: A small fault-bound graben sitting atop the high plateau surface above Fish Lake.

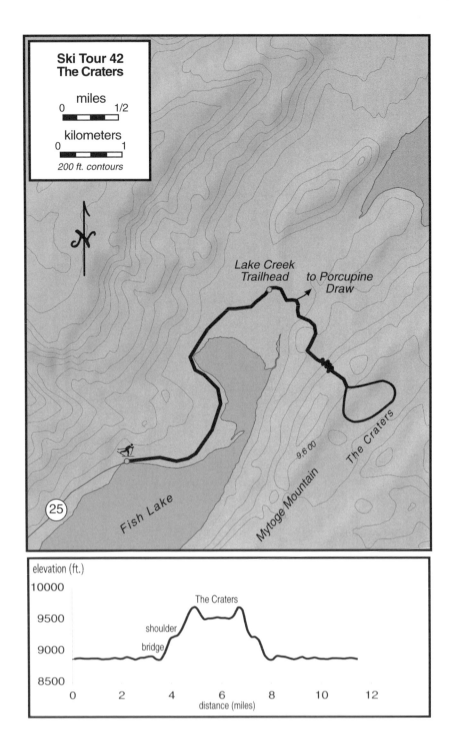

Other Useful Maps: Fishlake National Forest "Travel Map" and U.S. Geological Survey 7.5-minute Quadrangle "Fish Lake."

How to Get There (Fish Lake Area Map)

The parking area and trailhead for this, and for all of the ski tours in the Fish Lake area, is at the end of plowing on Utah State Highway 25 (Fish Lake access highway). See more detailed directions under Ski Tour 39—Johnson Valley Reservoir.

Ski Tour Description

The landscape around the Craters has an extremely puzzling appearance. Sitting atop the Fish Lake hightop surface is a small basin,

On the trail to the Craters

with two swampy closed-outlet lakes—not at all true volcanic craters. This small basin is a second fault-bound graben, with its faults running parallel to the main Fish Lake graben. The Craters basin is good evidence of the continuing tectonic activity of the Basin and Range migrating to the east. It is an extremely scenic ski or snowshoe route, with nice views of the entire Fish Lake region from an elongate rim atop Mytoge Mountain. This trail is actually ideal for snowshoers, who will have less difficulty with the steeply climbing section.

From the plowed end of the highway (generally near Bowery Haven resort), ski along the rest of the snowed-over road grade to the Lake Creek access to the Lakeshore trail. This trailhead is marked by a small turnout road and interpretive sign area from which the Craters trail begins. Follow the trail down into the swampy area, crossing the stream via a wooden footbridge, and continue up the east side of the basin. The Craters trail continues south at first (in an unmarked split from the Porcupine Draw trail), and climbs steeply up 400 ft. (120 m.) to a shoulder. After flattening out on this shoulder, the trail then climbs even more steeply through a number of switchbacks up another 400 ft. (120 m.) to a saddle within the upper surface of Mytoge Mountain. The trail then descends down a fast, straight downhill into the Crater Lakes basin. After skiing around the basin to your satisfaction, return to the trailhead via the same route.

Tour 43: Fish Lake Hightop

Tour Length: 10.9 mi. (17.5 km.) round trip.

Difficulty: Advanced backcountry tour. Serious elevation gain (2,600 ft., 790 m.!), the overall distance, and a few somewhat difficult sections of trail will make this a challenge for strong intermediate skiers, and more appropriate for advanced skiers with abundant stamina. It is a very long and arduous tour for snowshoers, but still within the range of the more adventurous.

Elevation: 8,660–11,282 ft. (2,700–3,440 m.).

Snow Conditions: Snow conditions vary greatly between years. Generally skiable from December to late March. Snow may be spotty at some of the lower elevations, but increases rapidly with the abundant elevation gain.

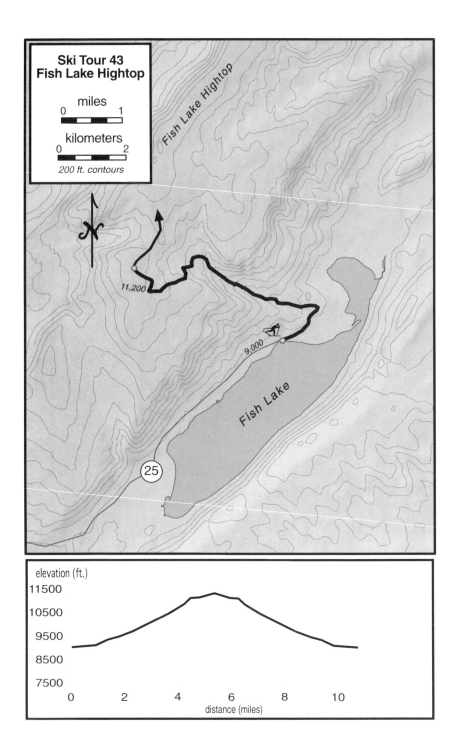

Geological and Other Scenic Features: Extensive views of the entire region from the high points of the Fish Lake Hightop. Good examples of the topographic effects of faulting.

Other Useful Maps: Fishlake National Forest "Travel Map" and U.S. Geological Survey 7.5-minute Quadrangle "Fish Lake."

How to Get There (Fish Lake Area Map)

The parking area and trailhead for this, and for all of the ski tours in the Fish Lake area, is at the end of plowing on Utah State Highway 25 (Fish Lake access highway). See more detailed directions under Ski Tour 39—Johnson Valley Reservoir.

Ski Tour Description

The Fish Lake Hightop is one of the most prominent peaks in central Utah, and is somewhat accessible on skis or snowshoes, within a long day's tour from the Fish Lake basin. From the hightop, one sees commanding views of the Sevier River valley, the Wasatch Plateau, the Boulder Mountain, Aquarius, Awapa, and Sevier Plateaus, Thousand Lakes Mountain, and as far as the Tushar Range in the south. The tour described here goes to one of the local highpoints on the plateau, although the highest elevation of the surface is farther to the north.

The tour begins at the Bowery Haven resort, which is typically the end of plowing on Highway 25. The beginning of the Pelican Canyon Trail to the hightop follows the Lakeshore trail, up a barren hill toward Pelican Point Overlook (see Ski Tour 44—Pelican Point Overlook). From the overlook, the Pelican Canyon trail climbs steeply up-canyon, through generally open country. This canyon shows the only real local evidence of glaciation of the Fish Lake Hightop during the Pleistocene Ice Ages. Glaciation is evidenced by the form of the U-shaped canyon walls, glacial debris, and hummocky topography of the moraine deposit at Pelican Canyon overlook. This may be something to contemplate as you continue the additional ascent up-canyon to the hightop. At about 10,400 ft. (3,170 m.), the trail splits, with one branch to the northern hightop and the second to the southern peak at 11,282 ft. (3,438 m.). The southern point is more accessible, and provides some of the spectacular views mentioned above. If you are not tired by this point, the hightop surface is an excellent quick tour all along its length (especially on a spring crust), with 360-degree views of the surrounding areas. The northern viewpoint sits atop a prominent local peak at 11,633 ft.

(3,545 m.). One may return from this point via the northern access trail (see USGS Fish Lake quad map for details), or via the same route passing by the southern viewpoint.

Tour 44: Pelican Point Overlook

Tour Length: 3.6 mi. (5.7 km.) loop.

Difficulty: Easy backcountry tour. This is a relatively short tour, with little elevation gain, and little requirement of route finding, making a good first introduction to backcountry skiing.

Elevation: 8,660–9,140 ft. (2,700–2,790 m.).

Snow Conditions: Snow conditions vary greatly between years. Generally skiable from December to March. Due to exposure, snow in some spots on the trail can be spotty and slushy in spring, especially along the climb to the overlook point. Heavy snowmobile use often characterizes the Fish Lake Highway, where there may be barren spots in low snow conditions.

Geological and Other Scenic Features: Nice overlook of the Fish Lake valley, and evidence of glaciation during the Pleistocene.

Other Useful Maps: Fishlake National Forest "Travel Map" and U.S. Geological Survey 7.5-minute Quadrangle "Fish Lake."

How to Get There (Fish Lake Area Map)

The parking area and trailhead for this, and for all of the ski tours in the Fish Lake area, is at the end of plowing on Utah State Highway 25 (Fish Lake access highway). See more detailed directions for Ski Tour 39—Johnson Valley Reservoir.

Ski Tour Description

This is a quick and easy backcountry tour, especially good after a recent snowfall. The trail ascends to a local viewpoint overlooking the Fish Lake basin. Snowshoers will also find this an easy and scenic tour, often best done with lightweight snowshoes in the thin snow conditions that frequently prevail, especially on the sun-exposed slope at the beginning of the trail. The overlook at Pelican Point sits atop a glacial moraine,

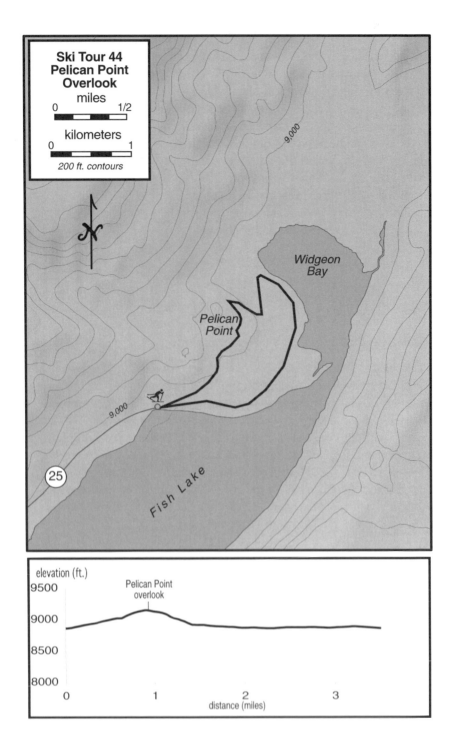

characterized by poorly sorted rock debris and hummocky topography. The debris was brought down by the relatively small glacier that existed in Pelican Canyon during the most recent ice age (Pleistocene).

The tour begins at the Bowery Haven resort, which is generally the end of plowing on the Fish Lake access highway. The marked Lakeshore Trail leads up an open, somewhat sagebrush-covered slope, at the point of which is the Pelican Canyon overlook, marked by a historical interpretive sign. From the overlook, descend a nicely sheltered jeep trail to the north, usually with fresh snow, in return to the flats below. From the base of this descent, one can ski along the Fish Lake Highway, which is generally used by snowmobiles, or alongside the road in the short return to the trailhead.

Tour 45: Monroe Peak

Tour Length: 23.9 mi. (38.3 km.) round trip.

Difficulty: Most difficult backcountry tour. If begun at Monrovian Park, this tour climbs over 5,000 ft. (1,520 m.), and will require a very long day of skiing—best done in spring. However, the lower portions of the trail may be skied very easily in winter to any number of stopping points (without going all the way to Monroe Peak). Also, with higher snow levels in early winter and late spring, the summit may be attainable with a much shorter skiing distance, by driving farther up the gravel Forest Service road. If the road can be driven far enough, this route is very appropriate for intermediate backcountry skiers.

Elevation: 6,200–11,227 ft. (1,890–3,421 m.).

Snow Conditions: Generally skiable from December to April. Due to exposure and snowmobile use, conditions in some of the south-facing exposures on the road can be spotty and slushy in spring. Snow lines may be higher, making the tour to the peak a much easier distance to travel. Heavy snowmobile use along the entire trail is common, especially on weekends.

Geological and Other Scenic Features: From the peak, extensive views of the surrounding region. From the trail, views into Richfield valley. From the drive to the trailhead, exposures of the local volcanic rocks.

Other Useful Maps: Fishlake National Forest "Travel Map" and U.S. Geological Survey 7.5-minute Quadrangle "Monroe Peak."

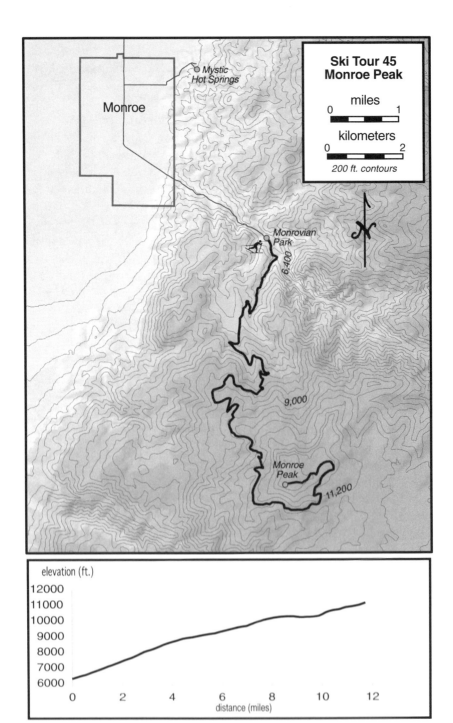

How to Get There (Fish Lake Area Map)

The Monroe Peak area is accessed from the west via Monrovian Park, a Rotary campground and picnic area about 4 mi. (6.4 km.) east of the town of Monroe. To get to Monroe, take Utah Highway 118 south from Richfield. Once in Monroe continue through town on Main Street, first south, then southeast toward Monroe Canyon and Monrovian Park. At the end of the plowed road near the park, there is abundant parking for snowmobilers, skiers, and people heading for all types of winter play in the area. During late spring, the continuing gravel road (Forest Road 078) may be driven significantly farther to shorten the distance of the tour to the peak.

If interested in soaking afterwards in Mystic Hot Springs, take a turn on 100 North, marked by a small sign near the southern end of the town of Monroe. Follow all the way to the end of the road at the resort (open 24 hours a day, 365 days a year).

Ski Tour Description

Monroe Peak is a very tall and steep mountain that rises sharply from the fertile Richfield Valley to the west. Although the peak is actually formed of an ancient volcanic caldera, and is therefore more directly related to the Tushar Mountains (see geological guide to Ski Touring Area 3), it is more accessible from the Richfield Valley, and more consistent with the Fish Lake area.

Monrovian Park is very much snowmobile country. However, at times these mountains can make for excellent ski touring, especially for those looking for some untouched powder in the remote region around the peak. Much of the Monroe Peak area offers wide-open slopes, sometimes deep with untouched powder, perfect for advanced telemark and backcountry skiers. Many such advanced skiers access the back side of Monroe Peak via the town of Koosharem (not described in this book). The ascent to the peak from Monrovian Park is a long and arduous tour, most recommended for more advanced skiers, especially during deep winter conditions. However, beginning and intermediate telemarkers will find a variety of gentle slopes near the beginning of the trail an excellent place to practice a few turns. The trailhead is easily accessible, and when snow levels are high, the peak can become closer than the 12 mi. (19.2 km.) distance (one way) from the winter parking area at Monrovian Park. Although the peak provides commanding views in this unique setting, ski tours partway up the mountain are still very much worth the climb.

This area is particularly attractive because of its proximity to Mystic Hot Springs, just outside the town of Monroe. This enchanted little "resort" has a truly unique atmosphere and is a great place to rest sore bones and muscles in a number of natural hot-water pools after a long ski tour in the surrounding mountains. The hot springs resort has camping, RV sites, "cabins" for rent, occasional small "alternative" concerts, and some very unique and natural hot springs mineral deposits.

From Monrovian Park, or as far up Forest Service Road 078 as you can drive, continue to climb the steep grade as far as you are willing to go. The road is easy to follow, and is generally tracked by snowmobilers, who tend, however, to be absent outside of weekends and holidays. There are a number of convenient stopping points along the way, and several sheltered slopes perfect for practicing a few telemark turns. The peak is over 5,000 ft. (1,520 m.) of vertical climbing from Monrovian Park, but is occasionally skied by advanced backcountry skiers. For those willing to do a bit more research, this peak is also accessible by a somewhat shorter distance (although a difficult drive on gravel roads), from the town of Koosharem to the east.

Additional Resources:

Fishlake National Forest (Loa Ranger District)
Local conditions, resorts, trails, campgrounds
P. O. Box 129
138 S. Main St.
Loa, UT 84747
(435) 836-2811
www.fs.fed.us/r4/fishlake/d2/loamain.html

Mystic Hot Springs
475 E. 100 North St.
Monroe, UT 84754
(435) 527-3286
www.mystichotsprings.com

Other Skiing Areas of Southwestern Utah

Beyond the Tracks and Trails

This book has primarily attempted to cover some of the relatively more popular and accessible skiable terrain of southwestern Utah, but has also made an effort to go beyond the usual touring areas and cross-country resorts. However, much more of southern Utah has extreme potential for real "out-there" skiing. It is worth mentioning a few areas that may be worthy of further exploration by skis, as well as other areas that may be skiable only a few times a year, and only during good snow years.

The Pine Valley Mountains, north of St. George, rise rapidly out of the surrounding Basin and Range to elevations well above 10,000 ft. (3,000 m.). This laccolithic complex is extremely steep, extending straight out of the deserts below, and deeply forested with aromatic Ponderosa pine. Although the area is a designated wilderness area, and therefore off limits to vehicles, the back side of the range (west side) is somewhat more accessible via a paved road to the wilderness boundary near the quaint little town of Pine Valley. A small, rustic lodge (Pine Valley Lodge) actually caters to skiers in winter, renting cross-country skis and providing guidance to the nearby trails of the valley. In many years, however, the climate is particularly dry, and skiable snow persists for only a few weeks out of the year. Much of the upper range is inaccessible to the average ski tourer due to long distances and steep climbs up narrow trails, often on icy snow. However, if the conditions are right, the Pine Valley Mountains definitely make for an excellent backcountry ski destination, within a very short distance from the growing town of St. George. Check with the Pine Valley Lodge for local conditions, availability, and trail suggestions.

One should in no way regard the few ski trails in this book as the complete extent of skiable terrain of southwestern Utah. Much of the remainder of the southern Utah High Plateau Country may be skied during particularly good snow conditions. Generally, areas above 8,000 ft. (2,440 m.) are skiable at least sometime during the year. Potential areas beyond the scope of this book include Checkerboard Mesa, in Zion National Park; Navajo Mountain, on the distant shores of Lake Powell; the Kolob Plateau and the Beaver Dam Mountains, both near St. George; Mount Dutton, north of Bryce Canyon; and even some of the canyon country of the Grand Staircase–Escalante National Monument region, when snow has recently fallen. Farther afield, skiing abounds in southern Utah, including great ski tours in the Henry Mountains (near Hanksville), the high LaSal Mountains (near Moab), and the Abajo Mountains (near Blanding). As some might say, "the fields are white, and ready to be skied."

Additional Resources (Pine Valley Area):

Pine Valley Lodge
960 E. Main St.
Pine Valley, UT 84781
(435) 574-2544

Dixie National Forest
Pine Valley Ranger District
192 E. Tabernacle, Room 40
St. George, UT 84770
(435) 688-3246
jhamel@fs.fed.us
http://www.fs.fed.us/outernet/dixie_nf/welcome.htm

APPENDIX

GPS (Global Positioning System) Coordinates for Trailheads

Trailhead	Ski Tours	UTM Zone	UTM Coords. (Easting, Northing)
Ski Touring Area 1			
A. Ruby's Inn	(1) To the Rim and Back (2) Forest Loop (3) Bryce Town Loop	12S	0398020, 4169990
B. Inspiration Point	(4) Inspiration–Bryce Points	12S	0396880, 4163570
C. Paria View Y-intersection	(5) Paria Loop (8) Paria View–Bryce Loop	12S	0397160, 4161870
D. Sunset Point	(6) Sunset–Tropic (7) Sunset Loop	12S	0397080, 4164420
E. Cassidy	(9) Casto Canyon	12S	0386680, 4177270
Ski Touring Area 2			
F. Cedar Breaks Entrance	(10) Alpine Pond (11) Chessmen Ridge Overlook (12) Spectra Point	12S	0339050, 4168760
G. Lightning–Navajo Points	(14) Lightning Point (15) Navajo Point (18) The Gnarly Grove	12S	0336440, 4172040
H. North Rim	(13) North Rim (16) Brian Head Peak	12S	0337990, 4169790
I. Cosmos Plaza	(17) Pioneer Cabins	12S	0337410, 4173900
J. Miller Knoll	(19) Miller Knoll	12S	0353060, 4170520
K. Duck Creek Camp	(20) Kolob Plateau Overlook	12S	0349890, 4153300
L. Mammoth	(21) Mammoth Cave	12S	0358812, 4159840
M. Markagunt	(22) Markagunt Lava Fields	12S	0345060, 4154720

Ski Tours		UTM Zone	UTM Coords. (Easting, Northing)
Touring Area 3			
N. Puffer Lake	(23) Puffer Lake	12S	0380620, 4241220
	(25) Cullen Creek Loop		
	(26) Lake Stream		
O. Elk Meadows Upper Lodge	(24) Twin Lakes	12S	0389810, 4243470
P. Highway 153 Turn	(27) Skyline Trail Loop	12S	0380460, 4242950
Three Creeks	(28) Three Creeks/ Grizzly Ridge	12S	0376760, 4240560
	(29) The Gorge at Three Creeks		
	(30) Strawberry Flats		
Q. Bullion Canyon	(31) Bullion Canyon	12S	0385620, 4252690
Ski Touring Area 4			
R. Oak Creek	(32) Oak Creek Reservoir	12S	0469750, 4216100
S. Wildcat	(33) Wildcat Pasture Loop	12S	0470510, 4219630
T. Steep Creek	(34) Steep Creek Lake	12S	0471420, 4210570
U. Happy Valley	(35) Happy Valley	12S	0470060, 4224510
V. Barney/ Griffin Top	(36) Barney Top	12S	0422470, 4186620
	(37) Griffin Top		
W. Pine Lake	(38) Pine Lake/ Henderson Canyon Overlook	12S	0410130, 4183600
Ski Touring Area 5			
X. Fish Lake	(39) Johnson Valley Reservoir	12S	0438460, 4268300
	(40) Porcupine Draw Loop		
	(41) Lakeshore		
	(42) The Craters		
	(43) Fish Lake Hightop		
	(44) Pelican Point Overlook		
Y. Monroe Peak	(45) Monroe Peak	12S	0406320, 4272140

All coordinates are expressed using the UTM (Universal Transverse Mercator) coordinate system. These units are measured in meters east and north of a reference for each grid zone (Zone 12S for all points in this table). Most topo maps (including USGS 7.5-minute quadrangles since 1974) are printed with this grid reference. Measurements here are presented to the nearest meter, but rounded off to the nearest 10-meter grid. However, because of the inaccuracy of hand-held GPS units (due to noise added to the signal), accuracy of the points here is no better than 30 meters.

RECOMMENDED READING

Geology of Southern Utah:

Geology of Utah's National Parks and Monuments. Edited by D. A. Sprinkel, T. C. Chidsey, Jr., and P. B. Anderson. Utah Geological Association Publication 28.
Geology of Utah. William Lee Stokes. Utah Museum of Natural History.
Geological History of Utah. Lehi F. Hintze. Brigham Young University Department of Geology.
Geology of the Parks, Monuments, and Wildlands of Southern Utah. Robert Fillmore. University of Utah Press.

Skiing Techniques:

Allen and Mike's Really Cool Backcountry Ski Book. Allen O'Bannon and Mike Clelland (Illustrator). Chockstone Press.
Backcountry Skier. Jean Vives. Human Kinetics.
Tao of Skiing: Aide Memoire for Cross-Country Skiing Aficionados (The Way to Learn to Cross Country Ski). Lise Meloche and David McMahon. Cold Fusion Heavy Industries.

ACKNOWLEDGMENTS

I would like to thank a few people for input to this book. First of all to all of those who have put up with my finding skiable trails in southern Utah, including Amy, Anita, Nathan, Grant, Jackie, Andy, Robin, Mike, Wayne, Tim, and Sarah, among others. Bill Murphy contributed a great deal of his knowledge of local winter trails and skiing history, particularly to the sections on the Markagunt Plateau and Tushar Mountains. My family has put up with my talking about this book, and passing them by on my many trips from Oregon to the southern snow. Nathan Wynn helped with photography, darkroom, digital imagery, and computer work. Derek Ryter was inspiring in the initial stages of this idea, and provided much-needed help in many aspects of the GIS work. The geological discussions and introductory material were greatly improved through the kind reviews of Dr. William T. Parry and Dennis Maw.

Jonathan "Guy" Wynn's fascination with skiing the red rock country began with his first discovery of the mystical winter scenery at Bryce Canyon during the spectacular snow year of 1993. He and his enduring ski dog "Allie" have skied southern Utah at every opportunity since, but have also enjoyed skiing the backcountry trails of the Wasatch and Uinta Mountains of Utah, the Pacific Northwest, and the Snowy Mountains of Australia.

Jonathan completed his B.S. and M.S. degrees in Geological Engineering and Geology at the University of Utah, and a Ph.D. in Geology from the University of Oregon. His geological interests have led him to studies of the history of ancient and modern landscapes in places such as southern Utah, central Oregon, the rift valleys of Kenya and Ethiopia, and the continent of Australia. He currently holds a post-doctoral research position at the Australian National University, and resides in Canberra, Australia—in strategic proximity to the vast ski touring country of the Australian Alps.